CITY OF ANGLES

For Bob & Joyce

Good friends & future
colleagues on the tube —

Al Martinez

4/13/96

ALSO BY AL MARTINEZ

Dancing Under the Moon

Jigsaw John

Ashes in the Rain

Rising Voices

Al Martinez

A N G L E S

CITY OF

A DRIVE-BY PORTRAIT OF LOS ANGELES

St. Martin's Press ⚐ New York

Design by Pei Loi Koay

Library of Congress Cataloging-in-Publication Data

Martinez, Al.
    City of angles : a drive-by portrait of Los Angeles / by Al
Martinez.—1st ed.
        p. cm.
    "A Thomas Dunne book."
    ISBN 0-312-13944-6
    1. Los Angeles (Calif.)—Description and travel. 2. Los
Angeles (Calif.)—Social conditions. I. Title.
F869.L84M37   1996
979.4'94—dc20   95-42862
                                          CIP

First Edition: March 1996

10 9 8 7 6 5 4 3 2 1

For my Cinelli and everything she is and

has always been, and for angry, funny,

tortured Jerry Belcher, who, I am certain, is

knocking 'em dead in hell.

ACKNOWLEDGMENTS

I OWE A debt of gratitude to anyone I have ever met, spoken to, drunk with, interviewed, written about, observed, argued with, read about, shouted at, gave the finger to, savaged in print, or merely passed on the street during the past twenty years or so I have been in L.A. Somehow, you are all a part of this book, just because you're you.

In less esoteric terms, I am in debt to members of the *L.A. by God Times*'s superb Metro staff for having done the initial legwork that furnished me with so many answers; to the newspaper's library for filing and storing the information so beautifully; to *Los Angeles* magazine for lists of minutiae that served me well, and to just about every other newspaper in L.A. County, from which I have plucked many little peaches.

I am further indebted to Lawrence C. Jorgensen for having written *San Fernando Valley, Past and Present;* to Gebhard and Von Breton for *L.A. in the 30's;* to Nikolas Schreck, who edited *The Manson File;* to Ken Schessler for *This Is Hollywood;* to Zena Pearlstone for *Ethnic L.A.;* and to a dozen other authors and editors who put together books on L.A. from which I extracted nothing, but just enjoyed reading. Perhaps you will also get nothing but draw similar pleasure from mine.

Last but not least, as we are taught to say, I owe fellow writer and good friend David Westheimer for his endless encouragement, my literary agent, Janet Manus, for her wisdom, knowledge, and absolute belief in my abilities, my editor at St. Martin's Press, Tom Dunne, for his awesome patience, and all the members of my family whom I love so dearly, and who can hardly wait to attend another book party.

INTRODUCTION

I BEGAN THIS book shortly after the L.A. riots, when smoke was still rising from mini-malls and gas stations in the South Central section of the city. Whole blocks were reduced to black and twisted ruin, looking vaguely like a movie set at Universal Studios. Sunlight filtered through smoke cast the neighborhood in the kind of half-lit amber glow that illuminates dreams and battlefields. Flecks of fire among collapsed buildings twinkled in the night like fallen stars.

It was a defining moment in the L.A. Experience. What went before the riots was history; what would emerge would be the city of the future, full of grace and peace and music and love. Oz combined with Brigadoon . . . or so it seemed. As it turned out, the worst urban uprising in the nation was only a prelude to other kinds of calamities, from wildfires to floods to earthquakes to the strange, compelling odyssey and trial of O.J. Simpson. There hasn't been any rest for us for one hell of a long time. Everyone keeps peeking in our windows wondering what's going to happen next.

I figured nothing could be worse than the riots, and still think of them as a division between past and present. But you can't ignore those moments that have thrown us into chaos and have placed our activities on the world stage, whether we've wanted to be there or not. We have become, God help us, a modern soap opera, with a cast of characters more intriguing than anyone who ever appeared on *Days of Our Lives.* Just call it *L.A.* and run it as it happens.

City of Angles is an attempt to view the city, not to explain it, although explanations are inherent in the view. So much has occurred in a short period of time that to define it and place it in proper context will require the view of historians a hundred years from now. I don't intend to live long enough to gain the perspective that would allow me to wonder if, for instance, the killing of their parents by the Menendez Brothers was a direct result of Lizzie Borden's influence on the history of child-raising or just another isolated mom-and-pop murder.

The best I can do is lay all of this out in a somewhat coherent pattern for others to ponder. If there are insights contained herein it's not because I have a special gift to perceive them, but because they cry out to be perceived. To one who's been around for a while, L.A. isn't that subtle. It's tough to miss what jumps out at you from a doorway and grabs you by the throat. You don't need a guidebook to find trouble. You've just got to spend a lot of time looking, and that's what I do for a living.

What you're getting is what I see: L.A. today. Now. This moment. After the riots of '92, the fires of '93, the quake of '94, and the floods of '95. A deep breath between disasters. I pick at random from the garden of events that grow in the smoggy sunshine, and in no way attempt to serve up the whole crazy, squirming, steaming, shouting bowl of urban stew, or to analyze its ingredients. I serve the mix. You taste the essence.

I call this book *City of Angles* more in deference to description than to the irony of angles translating easily from angels. I wasn't trying to be cute, only clear, with a twist. We stopped being a City of Angels years ago, but we remain as perplexing as the angles that comprise us, and the corners these juxtaposing angles create. We are many angles and many corners. Stick around, and we'll wander down some alleys. Bring a camera and a flack vest. This could get interesting.

CITY OF ANGLES

ONE

I WAS INTERVIEWING a woman who had just moved to L.A. from Chicago and was opening a dating service in a downtown office building. As we talked, the subject of her own marital status came up and she told me this story.

She had begun the trip west with her husband. He was dozing in the front passenger seat of the car one night when they ran into a fierce rainstorm just outside of Clinton, Oklahoma. The highway iced over when the rain turned to sleet. Their car skidded on an overpass, went out of control, and slid over an embankment.

The woman, who was driving, was miraculously unhurt, but her husband, horribly injured in the crash, died en route to a hospital.

"That's awful," I said. "What a terrible way to start a new life. Please accept my sincere sympathy."

The woman sighed. "It was just as well," she said, wiping a tear from her eye. "He'd have hated L.A."

L.A. EL LAY. LA-LA LAND. The Land of Fruits and Nuts. The City of Fallen Angels, of palm trees, smog, and kosher burritos. Aldous Huxley described it as a place of dreadful joy. Raymond Chandler said it had the personality of a paper cup. A downtown street corner evangelist named Bobby Bible calls it the Mother of All Whores. I call it Mom.

So welcome to the Mother of All Whores. Or is it? Good question. We'll get to that. Things have changed since the riots of '92. Even as I write, the changes continue. Old perceptions invite new distortions. Surreality has reached new levels. Truth dances with fantasy. Make-believe intrudes on actuality . . . or is it the other way around?

Even television wants fact-based movies of the week. High-profile stuff. Show me a one-legged anorexic choir girl from a good family who's raped by a U.S. Senator and I'll show you four hours on prime time. Give us truth, the networks cry. Based Upon. Well, Inspired By. Okay, Suggested By. Hinted By. *Dreamed* By, for Christ's sake.

Like flowers that grow where brushfires have raged, hope blooms in L.A. where buildings have burned. We have a new look out here, a new awareness, new energy, new hatreds, new loves, new passions, new power, new insanities, and new inanities.

Blend L.A. into Carl Sandburg's poem "Chicago" and what emerges is an intriguing mix of muscle and myth. Try it: *Script butcher for the world. Moviemaker, stacker of starlets. Player with plots and the nation's dream handler. Wheeling, dealing, signing. City of the smooth shoulders.*

Is that us? Part Chicago, part stage setting, part images on a screen, part something that no one can quite get a fix on? I wrote about a guy who produced low-budget, video-release movies that featured only women over six feet in height. They towered around him like redwoods mothering a fern. "This town," he said, gesturing to his Amazons, "has something for everybody."

I USED TO think there was no reality in L.A. I arrived in the summer of '71 from Oakland, where reality oozed from every alley. I looked down on a layer of thick amber smog before the plane circled once in ritualistic salute and settled into the murkiness. A darkness descended over the 727. We were in the clutches of hell.

I thought, okay, but below all the crap gleams an emerald city. I was Toto, hoping for the best. But below the murk there was *more* murk. Nothing gleamed. No discernible city lay at the bottom of the airy effluence, not even an Oakland; only a flat gray landscape of little houses that extended to all of the edges of the mountains that surrounded the place and to the rim of the sea itself.

"We will be living in a bowl of onion soup," my wife, Cinelli, said. "I feel like a crouton." She was on the verge of tears.

"Remember what Bob Hope used to say about smog," I said in an effort to cheer her up. " 'I'm not breathing anything I can't see.' "

"This is unreal," she said. "Have we gone into another dimension?"

In a way. The illusory nature of that introduction to the city continued when I went to work with the *L.A. Times.* I had come from the old *Oakland Tribune,* where pay was whatever the Newspaper Guild could squeeze from the publisher through threats and intimidation.

The *L.A. Times* was, and is, nonunion. Back then, money flowed like the Nile at flood tide. They paid all the moving expenses and even the motel bill while we looked for a place to buy. A reporter said, "Welcome to the velvet coffin." You went there to die in style.

My weekly salary increased by 50 percent the moment I walked in the door. There were fat yearly raises and bonuses. Where expense money was simply not available in Oakland, the *Times* forced it on its reporters. We traveled thousands of miles first-class for a single interview, stayed in the best hotels, and ate in trendy French restaurants from New York to Seattle.

Then we took weeks, even months, to write a single story and it could run to any length. It was a Writer's Newspaper, and a forgiving one at that. Witness the tale of a staffer who spent a year full-time gathering information on the philosophy behind and preparation for the Rose Bowl parade, and at the end of the year claimed a writer's block and never wrote the damned story.

An affable Irishman named Mark Murphy was the Metro editor in those days. It was a strange time. Reporters wore jeans and hip Betty Boop sport shirts. Copy girls with Hollywood tits and a waterfront attitude said "Bug off" if you got in their way, only the word wasn't bug.

Murphy took me into his small cubicle of an office shortly after I arrived and said, "Welcome to the good life. I want you to go to Montreal to see what you can dig up." It was heady stuff to a guy who once had to fight the *Tribune* city desk for bridge fare to San Francisco. Now I was off to Montreal to look around, to see what I could dig up. Why Montreal? "It's a nice place," Murphy said. I began to change, slowly, almost imperceptibly.

"You're getting weird," Cinelli said. "You wouldn't have been caught dead in a Betty Boop shirt in Oakland." Our marriage began to suffer. Unreality was tearing at my brain. In Oakland we wore neckties and caged drinks at a bar called the Hollow Leg. It rained in Oakland and we got pissed off. In L.A., we sipped pinot grigio at chichi little Italian restaurants and stayed cool, dude.

Then there's show biz. It permeates the city like spores in smog. It's a sickness, a dream, an element of the illusion. It's like everyone in Robert Altman's movie *The Player*. Waiters aren't waiters, they're unemployed actors. Every CPA is a potential television producer, every old lady has a screenplay, and every kid out of UCLA wants to be Steven Spielberg by the time she's twenty-two. How show biz are we? When Michael Landon died, we went into deep mourning. It was like the Pope had passed on, not a guy who played cowboys and angels on the boob tube. We banged tambourines, said good-bye, then canonized him. In Hollywood, the Holy Trinity isn't the Father, Son, and Holy Ghost. It's Michael Landon, John Wayne, and Frank Capra.

Every midlevel restaurant in town, from Encino to Santa Monica, claims at least one celebrity, certified by autographed pictures on the wall. "Great pasta, Mario! Julia Roberts." "My second home. Michael Douglas." "I love your papaya juice, Grace. Heather Locklear." "The best ribs in town. Magic Johnson."

At the big-time celebrity haunts, the paparazzi gather like hordes of wildebeests around the front entrances. A familiar face can cause a stampede. Sharon Stone nuzzling Johnny Depp? Feel the earth tremble with the thunder of the herd. *Rumblethunderthunderthunder.*

Ice-T and Dolly Parton holding hands? *Thunderthunderpushshovethunderrumble.* Madonna kissing Kissinger? *OhmyGodTHUNDERRUMBLETHUNDERJOCKEYPUSHSHOVETHUNDER.*

Places like Spago, the overpriced Pizza Hut run by Wolfgang Puck, is never without either celebrities or paparazzi. I was there with Steve Allen once. Jerry Brown came up to say hello; not to me, to Allen. The paparazzi must have been looking in the window because when I came out, they took pictures of Allen and the Ex-Gov and asked if I was anyone. I said I was Jane Fonda. A few of them laughed, but a woman paparazzi (a paparette?) said, "Screw you," but she didn't say screw.

If the feminist movement was not born here, it has at least reached its most glorious heights. In twenty years in L.A., I have been told to (fill in)-off by more women than I had been told by men in the preceding forty. Hardly a day goes by that a woman does not give me the finger on the freeway. *Up yours, Mac!* They call it the feminist salute.

My introduction to show biz came through Shortcut Benny Bernstein, who used to hang around the police beat. They called him Shortcut because in addition to knowing every side street in L.A., Benny also managed to take shortcuts through life. It is said he found a preacher who would marry him for nothing, a surgeon who would operate for half price to remove his hemorrhoids, and a lawyer who handled his divorce for a nice dinner at the Palm, a restaurant where aging pols and William Morris agents eat.

Shortcut never seemed to be employed but always had large amounts of cash. He claimed to have a law degree from Columbia University, which I never checked out, and made his living as an independent producer, although to the best of my knowledge he has never produced anything. But, then, a lot of independent producers don't. Much of Hollywood is a con. Success depends as much upon the personality of the "supplier," which is to say the producer and/or his company, as it does on his or her ability to supply. Mostly her, these days. Men are being phased out of The Industry. Women are marching in, and they're all taller than me. *Whatta ya got, Shorty?* Oh, God.

Shortcut introduced me to some people at a party once who turned out to be Legitimate Producers who said they liked my stuff, and I ought to think about doing something for the small tube. They painted glowing pictures of the possibilities, and visions of big bucks began dancing in my head. I increased my supply of silk shirts with pictures on the back and designer jeans and Mickey Mouse shoes with thick soles. I paid $150 for sunglasses because Elton John had a pair just like them. The guy who sold them to me on Sunset Boulevard wore glasses ringed with tiny lights that blinked off and on, but I wouldn't go that far. He was a somber young man with a round face that didn't fit the blinking lights around his eyes, which made it all seem so *tres chic.*

Show biz sneaks up on you. Like, 1974, for instance, was a time of cop shows on television. Prime time was choking on them. Good cops, bad cops, tough cops, sweet cops, bald cops, hairy cops, married cops, Jewish cops, country cops, and cops who lived on Lullaby Lane and ate tuna casseroles. Henry Fonda played that one.

I was writing profiles for the *Times.* So I say to myself, Why not profile a real cop? A detective's detective, a guy who is nothing like Baretta or Columbo or Starsky and Hutch or Kojak or McCloud. I discovered John St. John, Badge Number 1, LAPD Homicide. They called him "Jigsaw John" because he put the puzzles of homicide together and because, as a serial killer expert, he once solved a crime by matching the pieces of different bodies found all over the city. This arm to that socket, this knee to that joint, and so on.

John had only one good eye, was balding, mumbled when he talked, wore suits that shined at the ass, looked like everybody's grandpa, had never fired his weapon other than on the range, and had a conviction rate of about 90 percent. When St. John arrests you, one felon is known to have said as they dragged him away, you know you're guilty. John died a year ago, with an ego as big as his reputation. He even had his business card engraved on metal. It was all my fault.

I wrote about him for the *Times* as an example of what television cops are not, and television was all over me. It was part of the unreality that is L.A., the other dimension Cinelli had perceived.

Dozens of producers called. *Great stuff, kid. Just what we're looking for!*
Two producers took an option, I wrote a treatment in the style of a
short story (since I had no idea what a treatment ought to be), and
MGM-Television went for it like pigs at a slop feed. NBC loved it,
too. It was *Columbo,* but it wasn't. It was *Kojak,* but it wasn't. It was
exactly what it wasn't, and that's why they loved it. Familiar but different is the mantra of prime time.

Me, I'm sitting there listening and thinking I am probably history's
next Cecil B. DeMille. I have quit cigarettes, and am beginning to
smoke cigars. I have given up martinis for scotch. I am thinking
mogul. I meet Harris Kattleman, who is president of MGM-TV. He
says Call me Harris. I say Call me Al. It is a friendship that will last
forever, he says. Two years later I meet him in a parking lot at 20th
Century-Fox and he has no idea who I am. But back then, he says I
am the greatest and I will write the ninety-minute pilot script for
Jigsaw John, which NBC will air as a series.

I say I have never written a script in my life, I have never even
looked at one. He says writing a script is simply a process of setting
one's typewriter margins correctly, and he will pay $17,000. I say
I'll do it. I instantly give up cigars and scotch and go back to gin and
cigarettes. Writers do not smoke cigars and sip Chivas Regal on the
rocks. By now, I am also wearing red long underwear tops and tight
British jeans. Cinelli says I am going bonkers, but I am running down
a Dalí landscape and don't give a damn.

That's what L.A. was all about back then, see? That was the make-
believe part coming true, or was it? I write the script, they shoot it,
it becomes a series, and suddenly I am signed on with MGM, making an extra $2,500 a week above what I'm making at the *Times.* I
have the best of both worlds: journalistic respect and television
money. I work on another script and it too becomes a pilot that becomes a series. My marriage is going to hell. I hate that but don't
know what to do.

I have an agent now and a shrink, and I am self-incorporated. I
call movie stars by their first name. Then something happens. Harris Kattleman puts me together with Blake Edwards, who wants to
revive a 1950s series called *Mr. Lucky.* I watch the original movie in

a private screening room while sipping Dom Perignon. Then I talk to Kattleman. Everyone says he's a horse's ass, but he seems okay to me. But then:

He gives me explicit instructions on what he wants the pilot script to be. What he doesn't know is that I am recording what he says on a tape recorder under the yellow legal notepad I carry. Instinct says to do this. Harris says he wants a period piece set in the fifties, not a contemporary show. I say okay and write it. NBC sees the script. They hate it. They want a contemporary show. Kattleman calls me in and chews my ass and insists he ordered a contemporary piece. I play the tape back to him. His very words. Our conversation goes something like this:

He says, "I didn't say that."

I play it again.

"Harris," I say, "those are *your* words."

"I didn't say that," he says. "I said to write a contemporary piece."

"But the tape . . ."

"I didn't say that."

I stare. At first I think I am going crazy. Reality slips a little further away, like a tsunami sucking the surf from the shore. But then it comes crashing back in and I realize that Harris, like everyone else in town, is simply denying a level of existence that does not suit his needs. It is as easy as changing a stage setting or a line of dialogue in a script. I am so impressed with the man's chutzpah that I shrug and say, "Okay, I'll do it again." One does not debate spiritual transcendence.

I do the script the way he wants it, but it never gets made. Kattleman hardly talks to me the rest of the year. That's show biz. That's L.A. My two on-the-air series each last a couple of seasons and are gone. *Jigsaw John* with Jack Warden and *Bronk* with Jack Palance. I see them sometimes late at night. They also play in Japan and Germany. I get residuals. I create one more series, *B.A.D. Cats,* this time for Aaron Spelling. Everyone messes with the pilot script, like children splashing in urine, and it's a disaster. An old joke has a producer saying, "This is a terrific script. Who can we get to rewrite it?" In the case of *Cats,* everyone jumps in. One of the stars is Michelle

Pfeiffer. She doesn't mention it these days. When I turn the screenplay in, Spelling almost cries he loves it so much. When it all goes into the toilet, he won't return my telephone calls. Tears of love dry overnight in Hollywood.

It doesn't matter. I keep making big money for a while. Part of it is from a producer named Herb Solow, who comes up with ideas this way: We are sitting in the lobby at CBS, waiting for a meeting with the guy who takes pitches for dramatic series, when we hear from someone else who's waiting that our idea has been preopted by another writer-producer team. So Solow says we've got to think of something else fast so as not to waste the meeting. As the clock ticks off the seconds, we struggle to slap together a concept that features a rock-and-roll drummer who is also a private eye. We call the thing *Drummer*. It's familiar but different, challenging but comfortable. Fifteen minutes later, we have a script commitment. I make another bundle of money, but the thing never gets made. Good-bye, *Drummer*.

THE WHOLE TELEVISION experience clears my head and makes me a part of L.A. that is better served by the observer than the participant. No more Betty Boop shirts, faded British jeans, or Mickey Mouse shoes. I gain weight and my marriage is saved. I keep the agent and dump the shrink. Just as well. I was paying eighty-five dollars every half hour to a psychiatrist who kept trying to put me together with other show biz clients and work out a deal that would include him. Sometimes he sang arias to me to prove his talent, but charged me just the same. Another beat of unreality in the onion soup.

Now I write TV movies sometimes or episodes. I hate writing episodes. Like lions fornicating with zebras, episodes are not a natural function of nature. Writers should never have to write episodes. In fact, they are not written, they are organized in ritualistic sessions with producers and others whose presence and function are never made clear. One stands out in my memory. It was for *Jake and the Fat Man,* a series that has since vanished into electronic hell.

It began with discussions in a dimly lit room in the Black Tower, a stark, modernistic high-rise at the edge of Universal Studios. The room was cool and vaguely funereal. Sounds from the outside were muted. We sat in a semicircle, often in silence, staring and thinking. Present were executive producer Joel Steiger, co-executive producer (and friend) Bernie Kowalski, and producer Kimmer Ringwald. Had we linked hands, it would have been a seance. Old ideas tap-tapping on a table piled high with ghostly scripts.

Joel was in charge. They weren't crazy about the idea for the episode, which was someone else's, or about my handling of it. Suggestions for change popped like bubbles around us, followed by deep silence. During one silence, I heard a dog bark far off and wondered if it was a real dog or only the kind of background foley used in movies. Bernie or Kimmer would say something. If their suggestion was good, Joel would react and maybe build on it until the idea twinkled off into the distance, unadopted. If it was bad, he simply wouldn't respond. My ideas generally went unanswered. I was only the writer and probably one who didn't understand episodes.

Somehow the episode was put together over several such meetings and after many rewrites. I heard it went on the air, but I never saw it. No one likes viewing a decomposed body.

Half of L.A. has written episodes. Like a dog who deserves one bite, everyone deserves one episode. I meet old men who were old men when they wrote for *Dragnet*. It is the only episode they ever wrote. I meet others who have written hundreds. They still don't understand how they're done. That's because there is not an understanding to episodes.

The first episode I ever wrote was for the late Bruce Geller, who had created *Mission: Impossible*. It was for the series *Bronk*. Geller was executive producer, and I had worked on the pilot. I remember seeing Jack Palance standing around in the shadows of the soundstages at MGM. It was in the days before Billy Crystal and horror-comedy. I tried to give him a little humor in the script and he liked it. He displayed his admiration by staring at me from the shadows as I passed, his strange, gaunt face cast in eerie shades of light and darkness. I felt that at any moment he'd turn into a bat and bite my neck.

Geller read my episode and said, "What the hell you doing here? You've got the star in only part of the story."

I said, "I'm going for good story balance, where all of the characters interplay on an equal basis, and the story line is carefully ribboned through the interplay in order to create yet another level of balance that will enhance the total structure."

He said, "Screw balance, this is an episode," but he didn't say screw.

Oh, the reality.

TWO

Thou shalt not kill.
—Exodus 20.13

*Every murderer is probably somebody's
old friend.*
—Agatha Christie

*I believe people would be alive today if there
were a death penalty.*
—Nancy Reagan

THERE IS A theatrical quality to everything that happens in L.A., even murder. Show biz has a way of permeating the darkest corners of the civic psyche and celebrating those instances of tragedy that contain audience appeal. The murders committed by the Charles Manson Family, for instance, the blood-crime by which all other blood-crimes are measured, were exploited in both book and long-form television. Money was made by the sticky handsful because seven human beings stumbled in fate's way on a summer night in 1969.

Helping to make it an attractive property, if we can use the phrase, was the fact that one of the victims was a beautiful actress, Sharon Tate, adding glamour and intrigue to what otherwise might have been an ordinary mass murder. Well, no, I guess the Manson Family itself was peculiar enough to warrant more than passing notice. Chuck and Sue and Squeaky and Bobby and Sandy and Tex and the Gang were about as crazy as any writer could make up. They were their own superlatives.

We have much to choose from when it comes to making movies out of hometown murder. There are about a thousand homicides in Los Angeles every year, including those committed by some of the hundred thousand gang members that roam the city. Given the proper encouragement, we're likely to beat that figure every year hereafter.

We've got almost as many anti-gang organizations as we have gangs, but nothing seems to stop the little shooters from spraying the air with bullets, in both initiation rites and turf battles, and sometimes just for the sheer noisy hell of it. A reformed gangbanger told me once he had probably killed nine people during drug-enduced rages, including one when he was in prison. But that's all in the past, and now he walks the streets as a preacher during the day, and deals with his nightmares in prayerful atonement when the sun goes down and the silence settles in.

MURDER RUNS WILD in the new L.A. Contrary to the national trend, more people—1,554—were shot to death in the county in one year than died in traffic accidents, despite our five hundred miles of freeway. Another 6,500 were treated in local hospitals for gunshot wounds. The total of 8,000 is thirteen times the number of American military personnel killed and wounded in the Gulf War, and we're just getting started.

Those are just murder stats. Similarly making news are the cases of "justifiable" killings, the gunning down of a kid shoplifting or tagging or making threatening gestures or funny faces. You don't need a lot of motivation if you pack a gun and feel your life is being threatened. One hero of the day, for instance, was an unemployed actor-writer and lifelong gun nut who killed an unarmed graffiti artist he claimed was thinking of robbing him. Like others who have turned vigilantism into public acclaim, the shooter rode a wave of popularity among those who ain't-gonna-take-it-no-more, an outpouring that probably helped convince the D.A. to charge him with nothing more serious than carrying a concealed weapon. The dead tagger, by the way, remains dead.

Everyone owns firearms. I don't mean just the NRA guys either, who keep guns and pit bulls around their places in preparation for Armageddon or helter-skelter, whichever comes first. You can buy guns with impunity, at specialty shops, on the streets, in hotel rooms, in your living room, or at the corner candy store. A kid who couldn't have been older than fourteen tried to sell me a Beretta not long ago. He needed the money for a new bicycle. I suggested he keep the gun, buy a secondhand bike, and inaugurate the world's first bike-by.

After the riots in South Central L.A., you could buy a gun for the price of a modest lunch at L'Orangerie. The firearms had been stolen in the looting to begin with, and the savings, as it were, were being passed on to the customer. "Hey," as a street merchant said to me, "that's just good business." I suppose.

L.A. wasn't always this way. We long for the days we were considered, you know, kooky and mellow, before mellow disappeared down a dark alley. You could walk the streets then, if you could find a street worth walking. Tourists stood at the corner of Hollywood and Vine and marveled at being in the center of the magic world of movies. Hollywood had a mystical quality about it then. That's gone. Madness lit the night when the riots flared, damning the place where tourists once stood. Gunfire spat points of flame into the darkness. The devil strolled the Walk of Fame, where the stars of the famous are imbedded in the sidewalks.

Even before the riots, a hotel workers union, in an effort to rattle the tourist industry during contract negotiations, produced a videotape that suggested L.A. might be as safe to visit as Sarajevo. By quoting experts and authors in random sequence, the narrative implied that those planning to visit L.A. in the summer of '91 might rethink their itineraries and visit Orlando instead.

Union reps, amazed at the uproar their video caused among those who make money through tourism, said they were merely trying to point out some truths by mentioning the hazards of visiting L.A., including gang wars and earthquakes. The fires and floods were yet to come. The tape was intended as a collective bargaining tool, not a tourist alert, but as it turned out, the union's timing was exquisite. The South Central riots followed the videotape by days and two major Southern California earthquakes followed by weeks. I suspect Orlando did well that summer.

The same gimmick was tried by L.A.'s cops and teachers in subsequent labor negotiations, and will likely be utilized again by anyone reaching for tourism's short hairs. Labor leader Harry Bridges used to say when he was winning wars on the San Francisco waterfront, "When you've got 'em by the balls, their hearts and minds will follow." And so they did.

IN L.A., we look back on earlier calamities with nostalgia. Oh, for the good old days when Mickey Cohen was shot in a gunfight, when Bugsy Siegel was murdered in his home, when Clara Bow—the It Girl—screwed the entire USC football team, when Whoopee Lupe Valdez killed herself in a love triangle, when Peg Entwistle leaped to her death from the top of the fifty-foot-high "H" of the Hollywood sign.

The bad guys in those days weren't anonymous teenage gang faces wearing red or blue bandannas and driving by with Uzis blazing. They were people like Bugsy and Mickey. I wrote about Siegel not long after I came to L.A. The late Max Solomon knew all those people. He was a lawyer in his eighties who wore dark pinstriped suits with bat-wing lapels and a carnation boutonnière. He used to represent people like Siegel and Cohen. "You never called him Bugsy," Solomon told me one day. "He almost killed a reporter for the old *Examiner* for calling him that. Picked him right up off the ground so that his feet dangled. I had to talk him out of it. You called him Benjamin or Benny."

When the piece appeared, an anonymous caller left a message on my telephone answering machine. His voice sounded the way a pit bull would sound if a pit bull could talk. He said in a slow, measured growl, "Mr. Martinez, let's not be writing about Mr. Siegel anymore, okay? Thank you, Mr. Martinez."

I prepared another column and called him Bugsy several times.

"You'll be rubbed out if you use it," Cinelli said. "Do they still rub people out?"

"They waste them now," I said, "but it doesn't matter. I'm fighting for the people's right to know."

"To know that they called him Bugsy?"

"It's the principle of the thing."

I used it and wasn't killed. The pit bull never called back. Later, the movie *Bugsy* was made and no one was gunned down except War-ren Beatty at the Oscars. Max Solomon said I had balls and bought me a bottle of Jack Daniel's whiskey. I gave it away. I was back to a little white wine. "You guys ain't what you used to be," Max said. He died a few months later. So long, Max. Give my regards to Benny and the boys.

ABOUT 20 MILLION tourists visit L.A. each summer. In 1987, the year of our random freeway shootings, the number increased slightly, though it was probably safer to drive a Mercedes through Lebanon than a pickup through Los Angeles. It was like sunbathing in a hur-ricane. That they continued to come despite the freeway games played with live ammo should convince everyone that even death will not dent tourism. The new, violent L.A. will continue to attract the folks from Bald Knob, Arkansas, and Allentown, Pennsylvania, no matter what. Tragedy attracts and absolute tragedy attracts ab-solutely.

The riots started it all. Within a few weeks after the chaos had ended, sight-seeing tours were including the riot areas on their route. Tour leaders warned their customers they would be out of the area at sundown and put the fear of God into them by saying the buses would leave without them if they weren't in their seats by eight o'clock sharp. Other tourists in rented cars parked long enough to take pictures of the burned areas, then got the hell out. I talked to a visitor from Berlin. He said he had come to L.A. to see Disney-land, Universal Studios, Magic Mountain, and South Central L.A. *See the burned-out buildings! See the electronic stores once swarmed over by looters! See the red-stained sidewalks where blood once ran! See the bullet holes, see the little kids with horror in their eyes, see the unemployment, see the misery! Hurry, hurry, hurry!*

If Riot Land didn't satisfy an appetite for violence, you could tour the areas where famous murders occurred. Where the Hillside Stran-gler struck and the Night Stalker and, more recently, where Nicole Brown Simpson and Ron Goldman lay on the bloody pathway that led to her Brentwood condo.

My first L.A. serial killer was the Skid Row Slasher, so naturally I recall him with warm memories. He hit the streets in the late 1970s, doing in ten derelicts in the section of town just south of City Hall. Only after the first few were stabbed in doorways and down alleys did we pay much attention. They were bums, winos, no-goods. Who cared?

I began nosing around Skid Row. I found more than bums and winos. I found sad people, old people, disappointed people, angry people and people in deep emotional pain. They weren't all lying in gutters. Some sat in frayed chairs in the lobbies of hotels older than rainfall and stared out at the limits of their worlds through time-stained windows. Old men die in their rooms and no one notices until the rent is due.

I began writing about them. Since television copies anything innovative in the newspapers, the local electronic media went for the story like sharks in a feeding frenzy. Suddenly it was news.

Abruptly alert, the LAPD put an army of cops on it because that's the way they do things. Special task forces are set up, new commands created, new offices opened. Their temporary nature is not unlike a political campaign or a regional war, with the same brief flurry of activity toward a specific goal. That's the way it was in the case of the Hillside Stranglings, where each detective was assigned a murder victim. They were street girls, thirteen of them, who were tortured, raped and killed. A detective would learn everything he could about "his girl" and the manner in which she had been murdered. They became oddly close to the girls, and when the case was solved, the cops gathered at a downtown bar and toasted each victim with tears and booze.

"They were always 'our girls,' " a detective said to me. "It was never 'Victim Weckler' or 'Victime Cepeda.' It was always Krissie, Dollie, Laura. . . ."

There was no such emotion when they arrested an ex-burglar and Satanist named Bobby Joe Maxwell for the ten Skid Row slashings. The whole thing ended with a brawl between the prosecution and defense. A deputy D.A. said the defense lawyer had intimidated jurors by sending private eyes to their homes and probing the details of their sex lives. The defense lawyers said they did it because they learned two jurors had fallen in love during the trial and were living together. That, they said, jeopardized their client's right to a fair trial. The judge ignored their squabble and sent Bobby Joe to prison for life.

Thank God during our trying times we had a police chief willing to deal with crime in a manner that taught criminals lessons they'll never forget. That would be Daryl Gates. He created a battering ram tank that smashed open rock house doors. He demanded that casual users of narcotics be arrested, tortured, and hanged. He took Nancy Reagan on dope raids. He fiddled while L.A. burned. He refused to leave when the whole town was screaming for him to get the hell out.

And when he finally did leave, he took something of our pride and more of our sanity with him. Unreality. The beat goes on.

CHANGE IS EVERYWHERE in L.A., and we are forever looking for the line of demarcation that separates the past from the present. To some, it's the paving over of a drive-in where Errol Flynn used to screw teenage girls in the backseat of his purple Caddie. To others, it's the death of someone like Michael Landon and his ascendence to heaven or the retirement of Johnny Carson and his descendence to Malibu.

Shortcut Bernstein brought a page of the *L.A. Times* to me one morning and announced that it appropriately summed up what L.A. is today. He pointed to one story about a group of people in North Hollywood who claimed to see an image of the Virgin Mary in a Chinese elm tree. Then he pointed to a story just below it: Two policemen fired a total of ten bullets at a man who might have thrown a knife at them. Whether he did or not wasn't clear, but what was clear was that he didn't hit them. They hit him three times.

"How do you figure that's the new L.A.?" I asked Bernstein.

"Fantasy and reality," he said. "Before it was just fantasy. The Virgin Mary in an elm tree is fantasy. Cops shooting a guy who's got an invisible knife is reality. Go figure."

But we've always been that way. Images of the Virgin Mary have been seen on trees, bathroom windows, church walls, and even on a FOR SALE sign in front of a house that was snapped up by a Southern Baptist. Customers saw Jesus in a pepperoni pizza. The Virgin Mary was seen on a tortilla. Sometimes T-shirts are sold ("I Saw Jesus") or admission charged for a peek at a dusty bathroom window where God abides.

But like Elvis in a supermarket line, the visions are almost always disproved. The Virgin Mary in the Chinese elm was caused by a fungus disease. Oozing sap formed what seemed like a sacred face, the way drifting clouds take on familiar shapes if you stare hard enough. Believers were outraged at the very idea that the mother of God would be considered a fungus disease, but it did no good. The bloom was off the rose. Or off the Chinese elm. The crowds dissipated quietly. "That isn't to say it is not a picture of the Virgin," an arborist said helpfully as the yard emptied. Too late. Strike another miracle.

L.A. BEGAN CHANGING for me the night a face appeared at my car window. Everything had been fairly normal and crazy up until then. I mean, I never felt my life was in jeopardy, though my sanity might have been. Only once did it get a little hairy when I was out on a murder story with the killer still loose in a neighborhood. I matched his description and the cops began surrounding me.

"We're looking for a short Mexican with salt-and-pepper hair," a sergeant said, eyeing me carefully. "You're a short Mexican with salt-and-pepper hair."

The LAPD is not to be played with. I flashed press credentials I never knew I had. I'd have bared the pimple on my ass for ID if that's what they'd wanted. I didn't have to. One of our photographers hollered at them to leave me the hell alone, I was one of theirs. Press photographers have a way about them. The cops grumbled and went back to looking for the other short Mexican with salt-and-pepper hair. They never caught him.

The night that the face appeared at my car window was different. It had been raining lightly in the San Fernando Valley and the side windows of the car were speckled with drops of water. The face appeared on the passenger side. I was stopped at a signal in a remote part of the Valley at about two in the morning. I caught movement at the right corner of my peripheral vision. I glanced casually toward the window.

He stood there staring in, a gaunt-faced man in his late thirties, hair matted against his head, face pressed close to the glass. His eyes were fixed on me the way a lion stares at a gazelle from the tall grass moments before he springs. At times like that, sudden fear paralyzes the prey for a heartbeat that separates life from death, and I was frozen that way. I remember his face as though it's a still-life painting, hanging there in the misty darkness, and I remember that the lock mechanism for the door was up. It was unlocked.

Thinking about it later, I wondered if I'd been hallucinating, because the guy's face reminded me of a killer named Jack Santos, whose execution I had covered a long time ago at San Quentin. I was one of the witnesses crowded into a small room that looked directly through thick glass plates into the gas chamber itself. Santos and a guy named Emmett Perkins were being executed, and just before he died, Santos turned and stared directly into my face in the last few seconds before hydrocyanic gas sent his head jerking backward and spittles of foam forming at the corners of his mouth.

The face of the guy at the car window was like that, haunted and devoid of passion, a psychopath's face, where conscience doesn't exist. Side by side, Santos and the unknown man could have been twins. Or maybe they were one. What had I been thinking when the face appeared? Was I remembering the execution? Had I superimposed my memory on the window? Was it real or a wide-awake nightmare?

I still don't know. When I unfroze, I hit the gas pedal hard enough to drive it through the floor, and my 280Z shot away like a rocket out of hell. The face was gone in a blur of speed and panic. Who knows what the guy was up to? If he was real, I mean. Just another crazy wandering the rainy nights of a big city, waiting for God knows what? I talked to the cops the next day and no crime had been committed during the night in that vicinity. The guy at the desk said, "The shits are everywhere," meaning the mentally ill. The *shits?* That's a cop for you, guys. L.A.

After that, nothing seemed the same for me. I locked the car every time I got in it, and bought spotlights for around the house that turn on automatically with any movement. I was back in Korea when a war was going on, and everything that moved in the shadows beyond vision was a killer.

My mood didn't improve, nor did my attitude lighten, a little later when the Night Stalker was roaming the Valley. He was a drifter out of El Paso named Richard Ramirez who haunted the suburbs in the summer of '85. The guy was a bad dream, sneaking in through open windows or sliding glass doors with weak locks or no locks at all, beating, killing, raping, shooting, and sodomizing about thirty men and women. Thirteen of them died, and maybe they were the lucky ones. The others have to live with the memory of Ramirez coming in out of the night.

He was captured at the end of the summer by a group of people in East L.A. who recognized him from police drawings and brought him to the ground. Four years later he was sentenced to death, but not before telling the presiding judge, "I am beyond good and evil. I will be avenged. Lucifer dwells in us all." He's got other crimes to answer for in other parts of the state, so he sits on death row now, waiting.

Ramirez is a Satanist, too, obviously. He's got a swastika tattooed on his forehead and the kind of steel-hard eyes and leering smile that evoke evil the way a knife in the heart causes death. The face at my car window was Mickey Mouse compared to this guy. Ramirez was the very personification of evil. No sweet-faced Ted Bundy here, but a logo of hell I can still see in the shadows of my memory. He started out breaking into places to burglarize them but found a new sport in the sexual madness and murder he unleashed in the Valley.

As they led him out of court after the sentence, he was chanting, "Legions of the night, night breed. Repeat not the errors of the night prowler and show no mercy." How'd you like to have that guy sneakin' round your back door?

Television loved it. The day Ramirez was arrested, I got a call late in the evening from a network vice-president. He said something like, "We've got a miniseries here. I want you to write it, babe. Start getting stuff together, follow it through, and the minute the guy is convicted you can start writing. Who's your agent? I'll make the deal in the morning. This is big. This is very big, and you're perfect for it. Don't talk to anyone. You've got an assignment."

He called back the next morning to say the producer wanted another writer, tough luck, kid, he owed me one. He hasn't paid me yet.

THREE

ANY DAY NOW, as I understand it, Southern California will be rocked by an 8.3 earthquake, a jolt beyond anything that we have endured so far, the Big One we have been talking about for years. The earth will crack generally along the San Andreas Fault and dump L.A. into the sea. This is not a joke. It has been predicted by seismologists who say there is a high probability it will occur anytime between next Thursday and the year 3000. That is a joke. They don't have the faintest idea when it will occur, only that it will. Their predictions are as valid as a congressman's kiss.

When the earth does crack, Malibu will go first because it's right on the ocean and doesn't have far to travel. Ditto the People's Republic of Santa Monica, and then Beverly Hills, Watts, East L.A., Burbank, Hollywood, the downtown and all of abused, downtrodden, miserable San Fernando Valley, including Encino, where many television stars live who haven't quite made it to Malibu, the poor dears.

When seismologists discuss the possibility of a mega-quake that will wipe out Los Angeles, they salivate in anticipation, the way Pavlov's dog drooled at the sound of a food bell. Seismologists salivate because the very mention of an earthquake means television exposure. They are stars whenever the earth trembles to any major degree, strutting and pontificating on the eleven o'clock news like

Danny DeVito playing the Penguin in one of those *Batman* movies. They'll celebrate when the Big One comes and sends the Mother of All Whores plunging into the cleansing sea.

No one outside of L.A. seems especially sorry that this might occur, despite the entertainment value of our recent history. Just after the most recent prediction, friends invited me to a Good-bye L.A. Party in Oakland. They gave me a life-sized cardboard cut-out of Quirky Quake, a cool-dude cartoon character adopted by the Southern California Earthquake Preparedness Project. Everything we do in L.A. has to have a cartoon character attached to it. "We are a living cartoon," Cinelli says, "existing in a world of the probable impossible. Watch out, beep-beep, here comes the Roadrunner!"

DUE TO THE frequency of shakers here, we are vulnerable to every prediction theory that comes down the Hollywood Freeway. I am in constant touch, for instance, with a group of people from the San Fernando Valley who claim to be able to predict earthquakes biologically. That is, they regurgitate and/or defecate when a temblor is on its way. One of my regular callers is a woman who telephones every time she suffers a bout of diarrhea. Not only can she predict a quake, but she can also forecast their likely numerical rating on the Richter Scale by the degree of her, well, malady.

This is not a very popular theory in L.A. due to the disgusting nature of its methodology. To the best of my knowledge, no one has ever printed or publicly discussed in any of the media the Regurgitation-Defecation Theory of Earthquake Prediction. This is a first. I don't know any of the names of those who call with predictions based on this method (they wisely wish to remain anonymous), but I do recall one of them telephoning just before the last fairly sizable shaker and opening her conversation with, "I just vomitted on the lawn. There's a three-point-fiver coming." She was wrong. It was a 5.1.

Other methods of predicting quakes have included animals. L.A. ascribes mystic qualities to animals. That doesn't, of course, include Satanists who sacrifice them or certain groups of transplanted Asians who eat them. There's nothing mystic about a dog-kabob.

One theory holds that otherwise even-tempered domestic birds suddenly peck their babies to death just before a tremor of any kind. (Cinelli observed to this revelation, "It must be hell for the babies when a truck passes.") Also, dogs are supposed to howl just before a quake, due to the sensitivity of their otolithic organs. My own dog Hoover has no such ability, but we're talking here about animals of average intelligence, not one that stands in front of the refrigerator barking at the icemaker.

To show what credence we give to predictions, a State Assembly Committee on Earthquake Preparedness met in L.A. specifically to hear a theory presented by a geologist who claimed an ability to predict shakers by studying newspaper lost-and-found ads for dogs and cats. His name is Jim Berkland. He found that if an inordinate number of dogs and cats are reported missing during a single period of time, a sizable earthquake almost always happens.

I was at the state hearing during which Berkland was questioned regarding his theory. He explained that household pets are sensitive to earthquake "foreshocks" and depart in panic when the earth moves even slightly. That oversimplifies his research somewhat, but that's what I do for a living. I oversimplify. In explaining why cats and dogs run, Berkland compared it to someone saying, "Hey, let me out of here!" while fleeing from a swaying building.

Most humans, unlike animals, eventually return home, but that's a question of instinct, not loyalty, for which reason we similarly do not peck our babies to death during times of travail.

The committee chairman asked somewhat wryly where the animals went when they fled. I think he was suggesting there might be a kind of Bermuda Triangle for pets who flee in advance of a quake, from which they never return.

"I don't know where they go," Berkland responded testily. "Call Animal Control."

THIS HAS NOT been a good time for L.A., natural calamity–wise. It hasn't been a good time for L.A. generally, but we'll get to that later. The period straddling 1992–95 saw earthquakes, wildfires, and rainstorms that caused flooding and death. Now it's the fire season again and experts are already predicting this will be the worst fire year L.A. has ever experienced. That is because heavy rain has created lush vegetation which is now as dry as a watercooler in hell due to the blazing heat waves we experience.

Every time fire wipes the hillsides clean, we are in danger of landslides when the next rains come, which will no doubt destroy and kill innocent Malibu producers and bit players under tons of mud, as it has in the past. Then, because the earth will be soaked under monsoon rains, faults will slip and we will be victimized by earthquakes again. What the hell's going on here?

We have, in fact, just gone through one of those prolonged cycles, though not in that specific order. There were the wildfires of '93, followed by the earthquake of '94, followed by the storms and floods of '95. The storms have caused an abundance of growth that is drying fast, thereby creating a new fire danger. Meanwhile, it is also a good hiding place for rattlesnakes and mountain lions, both of which periodically threaten our already shaky existence, but they are the least of our worries, unless they form an army and march on Beverly Hills.

I came to L.A. the year after God tried to wipe out the northern end of the San Fernando Valley with a 6.6er. A freeway overpass collapsed, the roof of a hospital caved in, and a lot of homes, apartments, and stores were wiped out of existence. Sixty-four people died, and seismologists have been talking about the Big One ever since. While the one I survived may not have fit into that category, it was big enough. Its memory is a lingering one. . . .

JANUARY 17, 1994. 4:31 A.M. I am sleeping peacefully next to my wife in our upstairs bedroom. I am dreaming of being at sea in the yacht once owned by Aristotle Onassis. We are sailing in the tropics and a warm breeze is blowing across the bow. I am sipping a tall, cool rum drink with a tiny paper umbrella stuck in a square of pineapple floating on the surface. Cinelli is saying she doesn't understand why the crew consists mostly of young women in thong bikinis. I am about to explain that it is a requirement of Greek law, under whose flag we are sailing, that at least 70 percent of the crew consists of—

A deep-throated roar awakens me. It is something I had never heard before, a sound from the bowels of the earth, angry and threatening. I have barely opened my eyes when the room begins to shake violently. My response is instinctive and primeval: I think of running. But first, I reach out for help and find my wife's hand. There is no doubt in either of our minds what it is, but she clarifies by saying, "Earthquake!" It feels as though the entire bedroom, which is about three stories up, is going to be shaken into space. They will find us under the debris, a middle-aged couple, holding hands, and they will run it in the Metro section of the *L.A. Times,* page B3. Some will weep, others will wonder why we just lay there like damned fools instead of getting out.

The shaking is violent. I can hear things falling and glass breaking. Lights that I leave on in the downstairs hall and on the porch suddenly go out. We are in pitch blackness. There is a flashlight by the bed, but it has no batteries. I have been meaning to buy batteries, but I was going to wait until I stopped by the hardware store to get a new hose. But the hose we had was still useful so I put it off and didn't get the new one. Hence, no batteries. "Get away from the window!" I shout. It is a useless shout, since neither of us can get out of bed. My inclination is to pray, but I quit the Catholic Church years ago and can't remember any prayers, even the one about the Virgin Mary, which I should recall. I argued with a priest once because I didn't believe Mary really was a virgin. I was fourteen and knew a thing or two about penetration. He said I was an evil boy and would end up in hell someday. Well, maybe.

The wrenching lasts ten seconds. When it stops, I say, "Let's get out of here!" Cinelli leads the way downstairs. Stairwell book shelves twenty feet high have collapsed, dumping hundreds of books on the stairs and on the floor. We step around them as much as possible and reach the hallway. A few glasses have fallen from cabinets and broken. We avoid them too and head into the kitchen, where Cinelli finds a flashlight with batteries. She also finds a battery radio and turns it on. It tells us what we already know: there's been an earth-quake followed by a widespread power outage. More later.

As dawn comes, followed by other dawns, information is dropped on us piecemeal, like the shards of glass that litter our floor. The quake registered 6.8 and was centered in a densely populated sec-tion of the Valley. There were fifty-seven deaths, sixteen of them in an apartment building that collapsed. Damage would total in the bil-lions. The impact on L.A. was mixed. It brought us closer in way that the riots never could. Race wasn't a factor in this calamity. God was. We were humbled by his whimsy. Priests and pornographers suffered together. More than 80 percent of the nation's adult videos are made within a five-mile radius of the quake's epicenter. Their business houses cracked or went down along with the neighborhood churches. In the great cosmic design of things, rubble is rubble no matter what it's from.

Oddly, there was never a time when we wallowed in self-pity. We were never Nancy Kerrigan sobbing "Why me?" even though the experience scared the hell out of us. We bitched a little, stood in line for relief money, lived in tents for a while, accepted food and clothing handouts, and worked hard to rebuild. More than a year later, we were still rebuilding. Our house suffered no structural dam-age, just those books on the floor and some broken glass things. It was nothing to cry about.

Our good fortune was due to Irv. He was the building inspector who oversaw our remodeling project a dozen years ago, which added 1,500 square feet to our house, including the master bedroom. Irv insisted we put in steel pilings to bedrock, shear walls, metal straps, and a lot of other things that kept the old place standing when the earth shook like a dog after a bath. I fought him all the way on it be-cause they increased the cost of the project, but Irv, who was a man of few words, just said, "No pilings, no approval." Living in a half-finished house opened to the elements was not my idea of a good time, so I cursed Irv and had the work done. Twelve years later, the earth shook, the house stood and I prayed that God be good to Irv, wherever he was.

Cinelli got the garden hose and the batteries herself, and we have flashlights in every room of the house now. Seismologists, who are almost as popular in L.A. as agents and fitness gurus, dismiss the earthquake as moderate and get looks of longing in their eyes when they say the Big One is still to happen. I can hardly wait.

WE HAVE GIVEN the earthquake a kind of spiritual quality in L.A. We believe there is an Earthquake God. At Elysium Fields, a nudist camp not far from my house, it is said that proselytes dance naked by the light of the moon in an effort to prevent quakes. On the other hand, Shortcut Bernstein believes that all the humming and chanting we did during the period known as the harmonic conversion set up vibrations in the atmosphere that caused the shaker in '94. I'm somewhere in the middle. I don't dance naked and I don't hum or chant. Whatever happens isn't my fault.

In 1796, Spanish explorer Gaspar de Portola wrote in his diary, "Four violent shocks of earthquake frightened the Indians into a kind of prayer to the four winds, and caused the stream to be named also Jesus de los Temblores." Smart Indians. They never lost a skyscraper.

RAIN IS ONE of our more consistent natural disasters. It rarely just rains in L.A. It storms . . . tropically. This may not seem like a big deal in Miami or New Orleans or Corpus Christi, but when you figure a mattress in Lane Three can effectively paralyze the world's most complicated freeway system, rainfall is a major problem. Streets flood, bridges collapse, hillsides slide, roads are closed, and mud fills houses up to their built-in bars, especially in Malibu, where everything miserable seems to focus.

We have just endured one of those drenching episodes which, predictably, hit Malibu the hardest. A bridge collapsed, hillsides slid, roads were closed, and mountains of mud filled very expensive homes, the same as always. And, as always, the residents of Malibu, both famous and not famous, emerged from the muck proclaiming they would not live anywhere else in the world, no matter what, and sang as they shoveled the gluck from their living rooms. Nothing is very real in Malibu.

The big storms are always blamed on El Niño, "the Child" in Spanish, a climatic condition that occurs when a large area of water warms off the coast of Latin America and plays hell with the weather, from droughts in Africa to floods in the U.S. In 1992, El Niño turned the usually empty concrete-sided Los Angeles River into a twelve-foot-deep raging torrent. Four people died in the floods: one a homeless man asleep, or passed out, under a bridge by a trailer park that sent RVs tumbling out to sea, two in a slide that buried their home, and the fourth a fifteen-year-old kid whose face will haunt me forever.

The boy's name was Adam Paul Bischoff. He fell into the L.A. River trying to retrieve a bike and was swept downstream like a twig in a creek. A television cameraman was there and the evening news kept us hypnotized by the image of young Adam, his terrified face above water, his mouth forming the words "Help me."

Cops and firemen reached for the boy from bridges that spanned the river, dangling perilously from bridges, arms outstretched, only to miss him by a whisper. We watched in horror as he was swept downstream by the fierce current, a hand rising briefly from the river, reaching backward to where life still existed, and then vanishing. His body was found downstream the next day.

Even as the drama of Adam Bischoff was being played out, water-skiers were being chased from other parts of the river, boogie-boarders were warned to quit playing in flooded city streets, and surfers were told they were crazy to challenge the waves that crashed ashore along the coast—waves polluted with partially treated sewage from an overflowing system that spewed into the ocean. But they were hanging ten anyhow, dude, and because God watches over drunks and surfers, not a one of them was lost.

It's in those stormy moments that L.A. assumes an aura of unreality, as though we are in another dimension from everyone else, Adam dying in one and surfers playing in the sewage a few miles away in another: affluence among the effluence. Men and women jogged through the violent downpours in Malibu and Brentwood, played tennis in the private courts of Beverly Hills, and teed off for golf wherever a country club was open.

That isn't to say we are oblivious to human tragedy, because there's also a willingness for everyone to pitch in when the tides are running against us. Like Edward James Olmos braving danger to help restore calm in the riot-torn South Central section of the city, celebrities jump in to fill sandbags or man garden hoses when floods or fires threaten any community within the greater L.A. basin, then send checks later to help with the restoration.

Disasters bring us together. After the riots we were out there hugging blacks and Mexicans like we've never been hugged before, and I was personally getting damned tired of it. A prominent Latino name was a sure invitation for uninvited embraces, and because I'm a Latino name with a newspaper column . . . well, you get the idea. I understand the bubbling emotions, full of contrition and good will, *but hug me again, amigo, and I kick ass.* There's only so much of that I'm willing to take.

Never was humanity's symbiotic relationship more revealing than in Topanga Canyon, where aging hippies left over from the sixties live in cabinlike structures down the road from yuppie film moguls and furniture store owners in million-dollar estates. When torrential rains sent hillsides slipping, rich joined with the poor in filling sandbags and digging drainage ditches to shore up hillsides and divert the rushing water. Bottles of vintage Châteauneuf-du-Pape were passed around like Budweiser during breaks in the hard work, and I personally heard one aging hippie ask a movie director, "Can you buy this stuff at Pic 'n' Save?"

THE SANTA ANAS are haunting winds. They come sweeping down over the high desert full of heat and mischief, dancing like drunken ladies through the L.A. basin. They are wild and erratic and bring with them a sense of unease difficult to explain. One knows with certainty that when the Santa Anas come, sometime around Halloween, there will be a serious brushfire somewhere, and that means homes will burn.

I live in the Santa Monica Mountains, between the ocean and the San Fernando Valley, and four times in the past twenty years fire has come to my doorstep, veering away at the last moment, by the caprice of the Santa Anas in 1978 and fought back by firefighters in 1993. Flames as high as heaven, hurling their intense heat before them, crowning through the pine, oak, and eucalyptus trees, bear down with a terrifying roar, painting the night sky with vivid yellows, reds, and oranges.

My vision of hell is the memory of walls of flame moving toward me as I stood on the roof of my wooden home with a garden hose, looking across at a neighbor on his roof with a garden hose, with fire five times the height of our houses advancing toward us. Garden hoses against that? Fire filled all of my senses. The heat touched my face, the glare blinded my eyes and the terrifying roar of a dozen jet engines filled my ears. Helicopters and sirens added to the calamity. All my perceptions were of that fire and my neighbor silouhetted against the glow.

Not since the night battles of the Korean War have sounds and sights overwhelmed me with such totality, bringing with them all the mixed emotions of terror and bewilderment that combat evokes. Make no mistake, fighting a fire of any magnitude is war, and nothing our small garden hoses could have done would have delayed the enemy for even an instant.

I had covered forest fires before I came to L.A., flames that rushed through mountain towns tucked into the Sierra Nevadas or out in isolated sections of the Mother Lode. But facing one that approached my own home was a new experience. The moment I realized that a garden hose was useless against the fires of hell, I had to decide whether to stand my ground and be barbecued or run like a coward to cooler climes, and live to face similar decisions on other days.

I had already sent Cinelli, our children, our horse, our two dogs, and our cats away. All that remained in our household was me and a loyal but hard-drinking handyman. To the best of my knowwledge, he hadn't drawn a sober breath in the three years we'd known him, but there was an angry courage about him not to be denied. He had been an actor once, and I guess that prepared him for almost any disaster, because when the last firestorm headed toward our house, he insisted on staying and fighting it with me. "I'll piss it out," he assured me, with a burst of laughter that filled the air with his alcoholic breath.

As it turned out, God spared me, the handyman, and the house by shifting his winds to the south, arcing around our plot of land as though he realized a cowardly writer and a drunken handyman would be no match against his powerful flames. Thanks, God. I owe you.

AFTER THE BRUSHFIRES die, what remains is a moonscape of charred earth, blackened skeletal trees that reach agonizingly toward the sky, and a white powder of ash overlaying the land. I remember once standing before a neighborhood in the Santa Monicas that had been left in ruins by the previous night's fire and asking a fire department battalion chief if there were any specific ways of saving your home in a wildfire. I was thinking mostly in terms of new structural materials. He looked at me through eyes bloodshot from lack of sleep and said wearily, "Move."

Angelenos love canyons, and have jammed most of them with wall-to-wall homes occupied by minor television personalities and the daughters of failed politicians. Topanga and Malibu Canyons, much of which are in park lands, remain relatively free of that kind of suburban clutter, but builders and land developers never stop knocking at the door. L.A. city and county governments are the best money can buy, and builders are not hesitant about financially supporting their political campaigns and reminding them of that later on.

Topangans fought one proposed development for sixteen years and won out when the owners decided it wasn't worth the battle and sold the land, almost three hundred acres, to the state park system. It was a pristine valley of oak trees and green rolling hills with a stream winding through it, which is what attracted a series of would-be builders who talked about putting up a hotel, condos, mansions, a golf course, a helipad, and a lot of other structures. Everything but an NFL playing field and a space shuttle launchpad. The property ended up in the estate of a Walt Disney heir, and its executors finally decided that image was more important than profit and gave it up.

They were being fought to the death in arenas of local government and on the street and were being threatened with a court battle to keep the land from becoming a city of the rich. Topanga Canyon Boulevard became a gauntlet of anti-Disney signs, one of which was a beautifully executed image of Mickey Mouse giving the rest of the world the finger. It was too much for those associated even remotely with Bambi and Snow White, so they said take your land and shove it, though in a more genteel fashion.

Two examples of once-pristine mountain areas that *have* become Golden Ghettos are Laurel and Coldwater Canyons, winding over the Santa Monicas from Hollywood and Beverly Hills to the San Fernando Valley. Utilizing even the air space available, homes jut out from hillsides into nothing, perilously suspended on steel beams pile-driven into bedrock, as though that alone guarantees eternity. As effective as garden hoses against a firestorm, the beams will twist like taffy if the spidery fault lines that underly the mountains should send seismic waves pulsing along their circuitry.

Everyone knows that, just as everyone knows houses will die in brushfires and streets will collapse in rainstorms. Even minor disasters cause chaos in L.A., but we try looking on the bright side. As Shortcut Bernstein wisely observed one day when rain fell and houses slid, "There's good stock footage in that for somebody." Look for me in the next disaster movie. I'll wave.

FOUR

Oh! I'm packin' my grip and I'm leavin' today
'Cause I'm takin' a trip California way
I'm gonna settle down and never more roam
And make the San Fernando Valley
my home . . .
—From "San Fernando Valley" by
Gordon Jenkins

Anywhere but the Valley.
—From a postcard depicting a young man
hitchhiking north on the Golden
State Freeway

WHEN GORDON JENKINS wrote that song about the San Fernando Valley in 1943, he included a verse that said, "So, I'm hittin' the trail to the cow country/You can forward my mail care of R.F.D. . . ." That's because in those days, the Valley consisted mostly of orchards and ranches. It lay dozing in the warmth of its own detachment while World War II was being fought half a world away. Only the presence of an occasional movie company shooting a Western in the mountains and gorges that surrounded it seemed to rouse its inhabitants from a lethargy that was in sharp contrast to the debauchery taking place over the pass in places like Hollywood and Beverly Hills.

Today, the Valley consists mostly of unappealing stucco and wood frame homes, mini-malls, car washes, bank buildings, motels that rent their rooms by the hour, taco stands, hair salons, security villages, and drab yellowish apartment buildings occupied by people who speak Spanish and Arabic. With a population of about 1.3 million, it would be the sixth-largest city in the United States if it was one city, but it isn't. Instead it's an unseemly mix of rich and poor crammed together in three hundred square miles of neo-drab. Picture Wilkes-Barre, Pennsylvania, overlayed on Wichita, Kansas, and you've got the Valley. Even its disasters seem vaguely uninteresting.

Gone is the spaciousness that drew the first explorers about two hundred years ago, who, combining tremors and religion, named that small stream "the River of the Sweet Name of Jesus of the Earthquakes." There are still earthquakes, and Sweet Jesus is still very important in an area that seems to cant toward a Midwestern ethos, but there are no more idyllic settings, and the only river that runs through it is the mostly dry, concreted Los Angeles River. Trust me when I say there is very little about the Valley today that is bucolic.

Ventura Boulevard, its main thoroughfare, slices east and west from Universal City to Woodland Hills, a calamitous melange of coin-op laundries, porn shops, and all those other things I mentioned a few paragraphs ago. It's no Great White Way, that's for sure, but abounds in the kind of unplanned, strip-zoned mix one would expect in an area thrown together like a whore's wardrobe.

It is an endless source of amazement that all the small businesses that flourish along its seventeen-mile stretch could continue to exist through the worst of times. How many people buy picture frames in the middle of a recession? Who stocks up on shoelaces and shoe dye when the wolf is at the door? And how in the hell could a store that sells only trinkets from Scandinavia exist at all? As Shortcut put it one day, they have about as much chance at succeeding as a hard-on in heaven.

Everything in L.A. is constantly in flux. The Valley is no exception. Though it sometimes doesn't seem a part of the city, hanging from its side like a distended gallbladder, it reflects all the traumas that have managed to shake L.A. proper in the past couple of years. Gangs, for instance, roam the Valley the way cows once did, with the same kind of mindless resolve. They have come along with shifting demographic patterns that have created Latino barrios in places where once only white faces gleamed in the smoggy sunlight.

Part of that cultural tradition, alas, is the need for young men to prove themselves. Couple that with drug-created turfs and the endless availability of guns (a U.S. tradition), and you've got a combination that is proving deadlier by the day. Not all of the hell-raisers are Latinos, of course. White neo-Nazi skinheads find fertile ground among those who believe that, sure as hell, a war of the races is coming. Black gangs abound, and Asian gangs exist, too, involving themselves in shakedowns in the Chinatown section north of downtown. Boys too young to shave work as drug runners and sometimes as hit men, or hit kids, I guess, because they know that a kid, if caught, is never going to have to do hard time.

One of the newer felonies of choice, car-jacking, officially began in the Valley. Though it had occurred elsewhere before, the shooting death of an old man and the theft of his gold Mercedes in still shimmery-white Chatsworth sent shock waves coursing through our moral fabric. Those things could happen in East L.A. or South Central or even the Westside, but, by God, not in the San Fernando Valley and not with a man's gold Mercedes.

So Governor Pete Wilson came down from Sacramento, stood in the very place where the car-jacking had occurred, and compared it to something like a rape in church. That's the way we feel about cars in L.A. Cars "R" Us, Cinelli likes to say. There's a truth to that. Babies and old ladies can get shot down at street corners in the barrios, but start screwing around with ritzy family cars in the Anglo sections of the Valley and you got big trouble, amigo.

All of this is not to say that the San Fernando Valley is a swamp of crime and mediocrity. *Au contraire.* I began my column-writing years for the *Times* in the new multimillion-dollar plant built to house its Valley edition, a separate entity with a daily circulation of a couple hundred thousand. I had been campaigning off and on for a column, having tasted little licks of fame with the old *Oakland Tribune*. *Times* editor Bill Thomas wanted nothing to do with columns in the Metro section, but would tolerate my messing around in essay form in the suburban editions. So I spent four years as the Bard of Chatsworth, until a new editor, Shelby Coffey III (SC3), swept me into Metro and out of the sticks.

Over the years the Valley has gone from a nowhere kind of place to a nowhere kind of place with certain possibilities. Equity waiver theaters, for instance, are beginning to emerge, and so are eating places on a scale higher than Denny's where something other than chow is offered. It hasn't been easy. When a developer named Herb Piken tried to build an elegant $15 million mall in Studio City that would feature a restaurant called the Bistro Garden at Coldwater (the name of the boulevard), all hell broke loose. Neighbors yelled that it would attract drunks and bums who would urinate against their houses and tried to block its construction.

The restaurant was, and is, an offshoot of the famous Bistro in Beverly Hills, which for thirty years has been the dining place of Presidents of the United States, celebrities, and powerful studio executives, not one of whom has ever urinated against its walls, according to the testimony of the Bistro's owner, Kurt Niklas.

Elderly white people in L.A. seem to possess an unnatural fear of having their buildings pissed against. I think it comes from a genetic terror of bladder failure. A man in Woodland Hills successfully fought for the shutting down of a disco for teenagers on his block with the argument that at closing time, the kids did Number One in his yard. (He couldn't bring himself to describe it otherwise.) A woman in Malibu suffered from the same urinary neurosis. She lived on the beach and communicated with me through an intercom at her front gate. I was asking oceanside people how they felt about opening up the beaches to the public. It was my first interview through an intercom box. I felt like I was at McDonald's. The woman said she was opposed to making the beach in front of her house public because she had personally witnessed disgusting Mexican males urinating against her $2.5 million house. I had the impression she spent hours at the window, watching and waiting. "Thank God for the rainy season," she said, clicking me off. I'm not sure if she was grateful that the disgusting Mexicans didn't go to the beach in the rain or that the rain washed away the urine from the side of her house. I guess I'll never know.

Kurt Niklas was ready to chuck the whole Coldwater project, to, as he put it, "cede the Valley to Burger King," but I stepped in to calm the rage. Well, actually, I stepped in to stir the rage, pointing out that the new mall and its restaurant would be like a rose in a manure pile and the Valley ought to be damned glad to get it.

It was finally built, and seemed to pave the way for other chow houses of quality. *Poitrine de veau* may never replace pepperoni pizza as the food of choice in the Valley, but at least now you can dine nicely before being shot to death by a kid who likes your wheels. There are also a number of new hotels that have sprung up here and there, and office buildings and industrial parks, but they are not in a number enough yet to cause anyone to feel that the Valley is becoming, you know, modernized. Maybe it is better than it was twenty years ago, but that's not saying a lot.

IT COULD BE I am being a little tougher on the place than I ought to be. That is because of the haunting memories of the houses shown to us when we first moved to L.A. and were told that Woodland Hills, which at the time was considered the Valley's most desirable community, was the place to live. We didn't look like the Beverly Hills type and couldn't afford Malibu, so we were shown around Woodland Hills by a real estate salesman wearing red checkered pants, a yellow sports shirt, and an electric-blue blazer. The blazer had the real estate company's logo on the upper left pocket. He wore it like an emblem of honor.

The salesman took us to what he considered the finest homes in the Valley, which had sprayed ceilings with tiny sparkles in them in the living room and gold-plated fixtures in the bathrooms. He was a man who favored paintings of tigers on black velvet and who almost went nuts when the owner of one of the homes appeared. She was, she informed us almost immediately, recently divorced and, quite obviously, looking. Did we know anyone? She was in her mid-forties trying desperately to regress fifteen years through the wonders of layered makeup, silver eye shadow, dyed hair with a bluish tint, and skintight sequined stretch pants. It was obvious to anyone who glanced in that specific direction that she wore no underwear.

I thought the real estate guy would swallow his tongue he gasped so violently when he saw her. I was afraid he was having some kind of seizure until I realized that he was reacting to the woman who owned the home. In Berkeley, where a lot of women seem to lose their minds and their virginity in equal proportions, she would have been looked upon as a psychiatric outpatient, such was the manner of her appearance. But in the Valley she was what passed as beauty and desirability, and the salesman was standing on his erection. "Sexy Rexy," he called her later, and indicated he was going to make a special effort to win her favor by selling her house. What especially seemed to turn him on was her accent. It sounded Slavic with a French-Italian lilt, which I suspect she had adopted in order to enhance her irresistible qualities, along with the blue hair and the body crevices.

IT WAS AFTER that experience that Cinelli speculated aloud that she would have to leave me, burn her underwear, and speak in pidgin English in order to exist in such an environment. Unless I accepted those conditions, we ought to look for a home somewhere other than the San Fernando Valley. That's when we discovered Topanga Canyon, which is where we still live, in a house that has survived earthquake, fire, flood, and a lot of goddamn coyotes that keep tipping over our garbage cans and scattering stuff all over the street.

Topanga looms over the south side of the Valley, and is about as different from Woodland Hills as Nancy Reagan from Madonna. Herein, the last hippie abides among conservationists and rugged outdoorsmen, and earth mothers coexist with hug therapists, faith healers, and macrobiotic vegetarians.

It is a separate cultural biome, isolated by location and topography and the sheer determination of its inhabitants never to be associated with either the Valley on one side or Malibu on the other. One can drive from the Valley, through Topanga and into Malibu, in thirty minutes and be in three totally different places, both physically and psychologically.

Artists and writers and potters and weavers make their homes in Topanga, along with people who believe in inner enlightenment and visitations by aliens from outer space. At least that's the way it was when we first moved in. Film and television producers have found their way to the Santa Monicas since then and have built million-dollar homes that assume the apperance of estates. But, even so, they were attracted in the first place by what the Canyon is, and to the best of my knowledge there still are no sprayed ceilings with glitter anywhere in Topanga, although wall-to-wall carpets and walk-in closets are considered second only to the Church of Sweet Jesus.

I mention Topanga not only because it is where we finally settled, but because it represents the other end of a dichotomy of what L.A. is, a contradiction of airy wooden houses with high beamed ceilings among towering oak trees, and dank, cloistered Spanish-style bungalows in tiny, barren lots; hundred-room mansions like the one Aaron Spelling built, and dingy apartment buildings that are close to, but not quite, tenements; formless, floating, oceanfront palaces designed by architects, and predictable two-story Tudors in gated communities; the large, comfortable homes of wealthy Pasadena and the rickety wood frame houses of chili-flavored East L.A.

Topanga was a place where famous Hollywood lovers brought their weekend chickadees to cabins and isolated summer estates on land where the Chumash Indians once ground acorns or hunted deer. Old-time movie actor Richard Dix was among those who lured women to the mountains, in his case to a hillside down the block from me near a wash where I found a thousand-year-old pestle. A stone archway still guards the retreat where he made love beneath the towering oaks to the howling of coyotes and the hoots of barn owls, and perhaps to the ghostly amusement of the aborigines.

Topanga turned into a kind of cowboy mountain town after that, but went through a renaissance of sorts when it became the hangout of folk singers, rock stars, and people who grew marijuana for a blurry kind of living. In the 1950s it was a haven for those blacklisted during one of the most terrifying periods in U.S. history, the McCarthy Era. They shared their talents at hootenannies in outdoor theaters and waited for the political firestorms to pass. But the tradition of unfettered talent remains in the Canyon, with a level of tolerance unique in the L.A. basin.

There was even a Topanga Sound among musicians and an album

called *Is the Canyon Burning?* cut by somebody who lived there in the sixties days of sex, drugs, and rock-and-roll. The seventies brought new realities, and one of them was that you could sell a cabin in the mountains for about thirty times more than you paid for it. The Santa Monica and Ventura Freeways made Topanga seem closer than it had been, which attracted people looking for a quieter place to live, especially those with an artistic cant.

Cinelli and I came to the Canyon in 1972 and bought a place for a song (although it didn't seem too musical back then) that's now worth more than I could afford if I had to buy it. Efforts to turn the town into another Malibu, however, have failed. I still have one of the bumper stickers produced when an effort was made to combine the mountain and coastal communities. The sticker says, "Topanga is not Malibu."

MALIBU.

The very name evokes visions of lithe young starlets romping in thong bikinis along the golden sand, their tight, tanned asses reflecting back the sunlight like shields in the desert. We see twilight parties on ocean-facing verandas and the familiar faces of megastars whirling into a mix of imagination that stops the heart. Is that Michael Jackson? Johnny Depp? Sharon Stone? Barney the Dinosaur? The entire cast and crew of *Beverly Hills 90210* groping the entire cast and crew of *Melrose Place*? Reach out to touch them and they pop like soap bubbles in sunlight, such is the transitory nature of fancy's swift flight.

Joan Rivers once described Malibu as the only place in the world where you can lie on the sand and look at the stars, or vice versa. But that was the old image. The New Malibu, the one that has emerged since becoming a city in 1991, is a little more prosaic, hassled by the kinds of problems stars leave to agents and business managers. Its 25,000 residents, who once enjoyed a snobbery of detachment from the secular world, suddenly have found themselves up to their transparent halters in the mundane. That doesn't surprise me.

Malibu was born on a political sea of sewage, so to speak, and it still hasn't managed to reach any kind of permanent mooring place. Most of its twenty square miles utilizes septic tanks, the underground effluence of which, the county said, was seeping toward and polluting the ocean. The answer, it maintained, lay in a new sewer system. But those who ultimately would lead the cityhood drive yelled that a new sewer system would simply pave the way for excessive growth and destroy the rural nature of the area in the mountains behind the community. They mounted their horses, rallied the monied patriarchs along the beachfront Golden Ghetto, and got themselves a city.

The campaign provided a feast for cynics. Southern California intellectuals like Olivia Newton-John, Ali MacGraw, and the late Michael Landon, all residents of Malibu, spoke up on behalf of cityhood, and others poured money in the campaign to wrest territorial control from the hated county. The ecologically hip saw visions of marine mammal sanctuaries within the city limits and debated whether to make it a crime to harm a monarch butterfly, though it was never made clear exactly who might be doing the harming. Shortcut Bernstein, who rented a place in Malibu for a while, came up with a slogan for them, "Kill a butterfly, go to jail," but they rejected it.

The real fun came a year after cityhood when the first election was held. Twenty candidates were vying for three City Council positions, and during the interim from the time Malibu became a city until that election, new animosities sprang up like chickweed among the daffodils. High rollers began flashing big money and speaking up on behalf of their candidates, and the bitterness became so severe that the local newspaper began calling Malibu "Beirut without bullets." The chairman of Sony Pictures jumped into the fray and so did the chairman of the Walt Disney Company and the chairman of Warner Bros. Studios and the president of NBC Entertainment, all of whom lived in Malibu.

It was a time of confrontation among those who once had little more on their minds than what to wear, and it spilled over from the election to the community itself. In one classic squabble in Malibu's Council Chambers, actress Trish Van Devere, the wife of actor

George C. Scott, was speaking on behalf of continuing a strict ban on home construction.

A member of the audience, voicing his objections to her proposal, shouted, "You don't even live within the city limits!"

"I do too!" Van Devere shouted back.

"No you don't," a second man joined in. "It ends just past Charles Bronson's house!"

BUT STILL . . .

There is a lovableness to Malibu, a joie de vivre, that exists because of and despite its self-conscious worship of celebrityhood and all the accoutrements of money and power that go with it. Malibu, for instance, never riots. No matter what happens elsewhere in the county, or even within its own city limits, you will find no one burning down buildings or looting. Malibu's manner of manifesting its displeasure is simply not to invite you to dinner.

One of those held in displeasure for a while was actor Martin Sheen, who lives on a bluff overlooking the ocean. Before the area became a city, Sheen was named its honorary mayor. What those who named him to the post forgot was that Sheen is a social activist and has gone to jail a couple of time on behalf of his causes. So when he got the job of honorary mayor, the first thing he did was to declare Malibu a nuclear-free zone and invite the homeless to live there. That was about as popular as a fart in church and quickly rescinded by the voice vote of just about everyone within shouting distance. I pointed out in a column that if God had wanted the homeless to live in Malibu, he'd have made them television producers. Sheen's position didn't last long and he's never been named to anything in Malibu since. Next thing you know he'd be wanting to legalize marriages with dolphins.

Malibu will always protect its own image. Recently, roof rats were discovered in the Colony, a gated community of the real superstars on the beach just south of the village center. I saw one of the rats, and there was no doubt in my mind that it was a rat. But when I asked a resident about it, a matronly figure who was no doubt the wife of someone famous, she drew herself up and replied, "My dear, Malibu does not have rats. Those are badgers."

"They sure don't look like badgers," I said.

Without blinking, she said, "Even our badgers are unique."

FIVE

IT WAS MID-APRIL 1993. A co-worker walked by in the city room of the *L.A. by God Times* and said, "You staying in town for the new riots?"

I said, "Probably. We usually take a week off just after the first of the year and maybe a week in the——"

Then I realized what he'd said. The man, anticipating a return of calamity, was trying to schedule his vacation according to when the city might vanish in smoke and flame.

It was a year after the South Central chaos that shook L.A. The federal trial of the four cops who beat Rodney King was winding up, and no one knew what to expect.

When it occurred to me what the co-worker was talking about, I wondered if it might be a joke, like are you vacationing in Bosnia this year? But it wasn't. The guy was trying to determine (1) when I thought the new riots might occur, and (2) if I thought he would look like a wimp for being on vacation when they did.

I had fallen into the conversation without even giving thought to the possibility that maybe there wouldn't be a riot; but, if there was, it was hardly an event to schedule one's life around. One should weep over calamity, not accept it as a scheduled occurrence, like Easter.

And yet, during all of the days of the federal trial it was a foregone conclusion among many in and out of the media that there would be a riot no matter how this second verdict went, just as there had been a riot after the first verdict that pretty much said beating a black traffic offender was okay.

Otherwise-sensible people worked out charts on how far the riots might spread and whether or not certain freeways would be attacked and blocked by the rioters. Many stocked up on food and water and bought extra insurance. Some went so far as to establish backup homes out of the area, like rented cabins or motel rooms or extra bedrooms in a relative's house, places where they would go like hollow-eyed refugees from Anatevka, pulling wagons loaded with their belongings, fleeing from a war. Some just bought guns and waited.

Reporters from throughout the world gathered inside and outside the Federal Courts Building during the trial of the four policemen accused of violating Rodney King's civil rights. The trial on the actual beating itself was held in Simi Valley and ended in their acquittal, to absolutely no one's surprise. Simi Valley is almost a whole village of policemen, because it is reasonably cheap and far enough away from town to be gang-free. There are more blue uniforms in the closets of Simi Valley than there are in any other community in Southern California. It's a cop town with a cop mentality, and no jury in the world that came out of Simi Valley would be likely to convict a cop for doing what appeared, in aberrated form, to be his duty, to hell with the videotape.

Because a riot followed that trial, the second one, predictably, was covered with eager anticipation. It had racial hatred, it had violence, it had Hollywood, it had America screwing up badly. Everyone loved it. Reporters for the tabloids, both print and video, were loony with happiness over the potential chaos another verdict of acquittal might cause. Man oh man, there'd be fire in the streets of L.A. again, but this time the media would be ready. You're only caught off guard once.

At more sober journals, coverage teams were selected and placed on standby. The *L.A. Times* issued gas masks, beepers, flak vests, and cellular telephones to those who would be covering the riots. Everyone was asked to be on an alert status when the jury began deliberating. We were in a state of social suspension. The whole world seemed to be waiting for The Verdict. Dinner parties kept radios on in the kitchen. Reporters made love with their police scanners going. Photographers slept with their cameras.

Then it came, the announcement everyone had been waiting for. Well, it wasn't *the* announcement, which is to say the verdict, but it was an announcement of an announcement forthcoming. U.S. District Judge John Davies issued a statement Friday, April 16, 1993, that the verdict was in and would be read at seven o'clock the next morning.

We said all right, this is it. We kissed our wives and lovers good-bye, donned our flight jackets and, like World War II bomber pilots off to hit Tokyo, set out for a journey into hell.

L.A. NEVER DOES things in small measure. When we were laid-back, we laid-back all the way, flat on our backs, totally inert. When we debauched, we debauched on Page One with big-name actors, naked starlets, and the devil weed. When we murdered, we murdered in multiples that included celebrities, and drew satanic symbols on the wall in blood. So it figures that when our cops decided to beat someone, it was a lousy, racist, chickenshit, lopsided beating, and it was captured on videotape. That's just our way.

I was following an undercover narcotics cop around the morning after the videotaped beating of Rodney King made the eleven o'clock news. I was researching a column on the dangers cops faced on the streets of L.A., using a letter written to me by the narc. His street name was Dominic. He was a good-looking French guy in jeans, a leather jacket, and amber flight glasses. He had a bachelor's degree from the University of Nice. Not your average cop.

We were wandering through one of the worst parts of town, where drugs are dealt in what amounts to an open-air market on every street corner. Crack, weed, speed, horse, you name it, they got it. What prompted Dominic to write the letter was that a junkie/dealer named Crazy Lisa had tried to put a knife in his back one day when someone in an area he no longer works discovered he was a narc. She was charged with assault with a deadly weapon, but it was plea-bargained down to exhibiting a knife in public. She got thirty days and was out in ten.

"If she'd sold me a joint that day," Dominic wrote in his letter, "she'd have done three months. But she only tried to kill a cop. Ten days."

It was a good point, but it was overshadowed by the King beating. Everybody was talking about it the day after the videotape was shown. The radio talk show guys were going nuts taking calls, and George Holliday, the man who made the amateur video of the beating, was suddenly the celebrity he never wanted to be. The tape must have been shown a thousand times that next day from one end of the country to the other.

Dominic couldn't get the tape off his mind either and was saying the guys who beat King ought to have their balls cut off. But he realized too the futility of talking about good cops when attention was focused on thugs in uniform who had acted like Ku Klux Klanners. "Now everybody's going to think we're all like that," he said, "and I can holler my ass off all I want saying, 'Hey, it's them, not me,' but who's going to believe it? We're in the same house and nobody's going to believe we're not all the same kind of cop."

THE YEAR THAT followed the beating was bad enough, but not nearly as bad as the year that followed that, the year between verdicts. Everything seemed to go wrong in the city. A psychology of violence prevailed, and still prevails. Gang warfare intensified and spread into areas of L.A. where it had never been. ATM robberies, which is to say the robbery of people using outdoor bank teller machines at night, became a pop felony, increasingly accompanied by the murder of the victim. I wrote columns about not being able to walk at night in L.A. anymore, about the presence of fear that hovered like a dark fog, and about the horror of one month, an August, in which 263 innocent people were murdered. Letters poured in. We're terrified, they said. Save us.

Street violence dominated the media, both print and electronic, and word spread throughout the world that the City of Angels was a city of evil spirits, more dangerous than New York ever was, like Chicago in the old days of mobster warfare, only worse, because the mobsters only killed their own people and we were killing babies and old ladies and whoever else got in the way.

A psychologist friend said it was because of the climate of permissiveness that prevailed after the King beating. By participating in violence, the police had granted subconscious approval to brutality. Others said it was because of the racist nature of the beating, and blacks were responding by engaging in a kind of urban guerrilla warfare that involved the killing of as many whites as possible in the kind of helter-skelter predicted by Charlie Manson.

Even the weather got crazy, with storms and floods, the way it always does when there's a war going on. The skies seemed perpetually gray and the wind whispered "shit happens" through the palm trees.

Police Chief Daryl Gates satisfied no one with a relatively mild punishment of those under his command involved in the King beating. The feeling prevailed that L.A.'s top cop was more anguished over the existence of the videotape than over what the videotape revealed. His head was called for on a platter by Mayor Tom Bradley, members of the police commission, and, later, by an independent committee that evaluated both Gates and the LAPD and gave them a D minus.

It was a strange time. Gates refused to resign and suggested Bradley resign. Finally Gates said he would resign, but only on his own terms and whenever the hell he felt like it. He announced several dates, all of which he broke, and then finally, after a career that spanned forty-three years, stepped down and out. Now he's a radio talk show host. Bradley later also said he would not pursue the job of mayor for a sixth consecutive term. It was time. Conflict-of-interest charges and friends in legal trouble were dogging his footsteps, and the footsteps were getting harder and harder to take for the seventy-two-year-old mayor. L.A. was going to hell, and he wasn't about to go with it. Neither was the D.A., who announced he wouldn't seek reelection, or the superintendent of schools, who said he'd had it, too.

L.A. was a city everyone was getting the hell out of.

AS IT TURNED OUT, they could have stayed. The verdict in the federal trial wasn't bad at all. Koon and Powell guilty, Wind and Briseno innocent. The smirking sergeant in charge who had made racist jokes and the guy who did all the club-swinging, nailed and off to prison. The other two, off the hook. A split decision. There were those who said it was meant to please everyone. It pretty much did.

The town was ready to be pleased. We'd been hanging from a cliff for a year, ever since the riot in South Central. Or what we later came to regard as the civil unrest or urban disorder or the uprising. Some said it was a revolution, others therapy. There was a lot of killing and a lot of looting. Later, a few of the looters gave stuff back. But the dead stayed dead.

The Reginald Denny beating trial started about the same time as that of the four cops, but got delayed. Denny is the white guy whose truck got stalled at Florence and Normandie, the epicenter of the riot. He was pulled out and damned near beaten to death by black thugs. Two men, Damian Williams and Henry Watson, were charged with attempted murder and a lot of other things. The beating was captured on tape by a television helicopter cameraman who'd been listening to a police scanner. Video-reality again. I suspect the delay in his beating trial was deliberate. If the white cops had gotten acquitted of beating a black guy and the black thugs had gotten convicted of beating a white guy, there would have really been hell to pay. There might've even been hell to pay the other way around, as Cinelli pointed out. They might've rioted in Beverly Hills. "Count me in if they do," she said. "I'm looting at Tiffany's."

The attempted-murder charges against Williams and Watson were thrown out by a jury. They got convicted on lesser counts. Denny said he was happy. I guess everyone else was, too.

I COVERED THE riots. I didn't have a gas mask or a beeper or a helmet or a flak vest or even a cellular phone, just a notebook. It was blue. And I had a pen. And I had questions. I was from the era when reporters didn't have a lot of protection. We had to damned well keep our asses down and look out for ourselves and sometimes for our photographers, who were always concentrating on the action and moving in for a close-up and not looking at who might be shooting in their direction. They had a tendency to back off of cliffs while trying to get the right focus or composition to their picture.

The Berkeley riots in the sixties were like that. I was there, too— a journalistic riot buff who just can't get enough of that wonderful stuff. There were all kinds of gunfire and billows of teargas you had to avoid if possible and cops who would have loved to stick a .38 up a reporter's behind. There were similarities in South Central, although since the cops weren't there right away, it was the rioters you had to watch out for. You know the story. Gates wasn't talking to Bradley nor Bradley to Gates, so there was zero communication when those first pictures of the burnings and beatings began appearing on television.

The chief was at a fund-raising dinner and the mayor was at church, and damned if they were going to leave. Cops I know on a command level screamed their bloody heads off into their radios to get some people to the riot areas, but word had to come from the top, and it hadn't. I stood back and watched the rioters move in waves of humanity from store to store, smashing and looting, with a self-sustaining turbulence that seemed to grow by the minute, like a firestorm in dry brush.

I LOOK INTO *one sweaty black face and it looks back, and I see frustration there and a sort of redemptive glory that says the fire has been a long time com-*

ing. *"Why are you doing this?"* I ask. *"Why are you burning down your own neighborhood?"* He is a husky teenager who wears his Dodgers cap backward. Before that became a style, it was a warning: Don't mess with me. *"We have to show our rage,"* he says. *"We have to do something."* Flames claw skyward like living animals, smoke billows over the angry ghetto. *"Let me get this straight,"* I say. *"You can't articulate your rage, so you burn down your house? What am I missing here?"* My son Allen, a talented photographer, is with me taking pictures. My aggressive manner makes him nervous. Where the hell do I think I am, on **60 Minutes?** *"What do you want us to do,"* the kid replies angrily, *"catch a bus to North Hollywood?"* He disappears into the smoke like an apparition, and I hear his voice drifting back. He says, *"Get out of here while you can!"* and means it.

THE COPS FINALLY came and then the National Guard, with guns and bayonets and a determination to make up for what they hadn't done in the first place. An exhausted serenity followed. We were like long-distance runners after a race, walking in circles, blank-eyed, trying to catch our breath, the roar of the crowd gone silent, the excitement past.

When it was over, we talked about healing and sang about atonement and forgave just about every killing, looting, store-burning, bottle-throwing, cop-hating son of a bitch who came down the pike. Every politician and political candidate from Bill Clinton to Pat Buchanan came to town to look, shake their heads, and say how awful, how inappropriate, how utterly unfortunate, and everyone promised the blacks in the 'hoods we'd make up for all their anguish. Then we appointed a white guy from Orange County to rebuild their community.

A year later, it still wasn't rebuilt and the white guy, that would be Peter Ueberroth, the *wunderkind* of the '84 Olympics, quit the leadership in frustration to-spend-more-time-with-my-family. I suspect there just wasn't enough glory in the job, the way there was when he headed the '84 Olympics or when he was commissioner of baseball. There are no standing ovations in the ghetto.

SIX

MIDNIGHT. I AM driving the Santa Monica Freeway west out of downtown. The new towers of L.A. are behind me, lit up in the velvety spring darkness like a corner of Manhattan; a small corner, to be sure, but a skyline nonetheless. Twenty years ago, there was still a thirteen-story limit on any building, imposed by an earthquake-frightened municipal government that foresaw calamity in height. There was no downtown skyline when I came here in 1972. But once the height ban was lifted, the towers rose—and continue to rise—like weeds in a prairie, adding a new dimension to a city that used to be horizontal.

The night is as warm and sweet as a baby's kiss, but it bristles with tension. I listen to two news radio stations, switching from one to the other, alert for any signs of disturbance in the city. They repeat the same news again and again, underplaying the possibilities of chaos in a display of self-restraint rarely seen in a competition-intense radio market. My destination is South Central. I'll pull off at Western and head toward Slauson. It was the apex of the riots in '92 and could be again in '93. It is Friday, April 17. In approximately seven hours, a Federal jury will announce that second verdict in the beating case of Rodney King.

I am looking at the city in the simmering hours before what could be a second elevation of hell through the wide streets and cracked sidewalks of the black ghettos of L.A. Cinelli is with me. I don't usually bring my wife on stories that hint of peril, but she insisted that this was a part of her life, too. Women are not to be denied their place in a new world of shifting demographics, though armies hide behind dark corners of change. She doesn't have to be here, but then neither do I. I'm a columnist, and the duty of the columnist, as a wise man once remarked, is to arrive *after* the battle and shoot the wounded. But I'm also a street kid from East Oakland, a reporter for twenty-four years before and between column-writing episodes on two newspapers, and it seems perfectly natural to be in the center of hellfire.

"There's a kind of uneasy feeling to the night," Cinelli is saying as I drive west on an oddly empty freeway, occasionally scanning the horizon for signs of fire. It is a rare time in L.A. when the ribbons of concrete that connect us are so quiet, regardless of the time of day . . . or night. "Remember when we were in Africa and the lions were wandering through the campsite? How still and silent and unnerving it was?" I remember. We were camped on the edge of the Masai Mara in an area never before utilized as a campsite. What we didn't know until night came was that it was the turf of a pride of fifteen lions. At the first sign of darkness, when their hunting hours began, they appeared on the periphery of the site, yellow eyes glowing like specks of amber. As night deepened, they invaded the camping area, prowling around the tightly zippered tents, defying efforts of the safari-leader in a Land Rover to chase them off, rarely making a sound, but present until dawn.

There is that feeling this night, that something is out there, ready to spring, ready to spill blood with claws configured into guns and knives and clubs. I am thinking of the lions when I spot flames rising into the sky off Vermont. Cinelli sees them at the same time and says, "Here we go." There is the tightness in her voice of a warrior who looks down from the hilltop for the first time and sees a valley filled with the enemy coming his way. I glance at her. She can't keep her eyes off the fire.

Streets that nestle up to the freeways of Los Angeles are chopped into one- and two-block segments that often do not connect and end up going nowhere. The streets came first and the freeways were laid upon existing neighborhoods, slicing up major and minor thoroughfares alike, dissecting communities and creating separate social and sometimes cultural biomes, like separate squares in a checkerboard pattern.

When I pull off Vermont, looking for the source of the flames, I confront the result of the chopping and slicing. I am in a maze, seeing the fire in the distance but unable to reach it, driving down darkened streets that end abruptly, watched by eyes that peer from dust-streaked windows and by groups of men gathered near the steps of wood frame homes built in the depressed thirties. I wonder why anyone would be up and out past midnight for no obvious reason, hanging around a darkened home on a street without lights, but I don't wait around to find out. There is a shiver of danger in the air, an almost palpable presence on the kinds of streets that do not tempt tourism.

It takes fifteen long minutes to find my way to the fire, and when I do, it is anticlimactic. A car has been burning, and the crews of two fire engines have all but extinguished the flames. A highway patrol car is parked off to one side. Locals, some in nightclothes, gather in clusters nearby, curious but not hostile. The highway patrol officer is a woman who seems too petite to be wearing the gun slung at her side, appearing somehow like a child in grown-up clothes. She is ill at ease in the environment and is glad to see the press credentials hung around my neck.

"It's nothing," she says, anticipating my question. A television van squeals around a corner and parks behind my car. "Just a car fire." As I walk away, she's saying the same thing to the TV reporter, an eager young man who writes furiously in a notebook, praying that this too can play a role in whatever the night, and the morning, may hold.

THERE ARE NO tenements in South Central Los Angeles, and none in the city itself. One can find substandard hotels jammed with those unable to afford better accommodations, usually Latinos. They are rat- and cockroach-infested hovels that leak when it rains, their inhabitants chilled in the winter and smothered by heat in the blazing summers. But the buildings are found in individual, isolated locations, not squeezed together side by side in awesome rows of abject poverty, the way they are in New York and Chicago. Give us that much at least.

The working poor in South Central live in small wood-frame or stucco homes with porches and shuttered windows, built before World War II, when L.A. was relatively at peace with itself. An addition to the homes in more recent times have been cyclone fences around their yards, metal bars on windows, and double dead bolts on doors. This is gangland, the split turfs of the Bloods and the Crips, and trouble abounds. Many of the homes are pocked by bullet holes, and the hieroglyphics of graffiti spell danger across the face of the neighborhood.

I see these homes in the post-midnight gloom that Saturday in April and, hours later, by dawn's first light. Cinelli and I cruise the area for two hours. It remains strangely silent for a Friday night. Few pedestrians are on the sidewalks and traffic is light on the main thoroughfares. There are no shouts to herald the weekend, no sirens, no gunshots, no angry voices. The many liquor stores that exist in South Central are brightly lit, but no crowds gather near the front doors. No young thugs cruise the streets. And though 2,500 policemen and 600 National Guardsmen stand ready to quell any disturbances, they remain out of sight, waiting. South Central lies like wounded prey, too frightened to move, expecting the worst.

DAWN BRINGS A gentler time. Even with the verdict still hanging over its head like the Sword of Damocles, much of the tension seems to have drained from L.A. It's a feeling I get as I drive along Pacific Coast Highway out of Topanga Canyon. Not that one would expect trouble here. This is about as remote from any scene of urban combat as Oakland from Shangri-la. But, still, the traffic is normal and the news mundane and the city has slept through its tension without firing a shot. There is a sweetness to the morning that defies violence, and I hope for the best as I pick up the freeway toward South Central.

I am alone this time. If it happens that I am to be in the middle of a riot, I want to be there without fearing for the safety of a lifelong companion. It's about 6 A.M., an hour removed from the time of the Rodney King verdict. I am heading for the home of a black woman who, with her granddaughter, lives in the middle of South Central. Her name is Diane Chapman. Her granddaughter is Trulysia. Theirs is one of the homes riddled by bullets from prior gang wars, an otherwise neat stucco house Chapman has occupied for twenty-three years. This was a quiet neighborhood once, rooted in the simple family values that existed a long time ago. I come from a neighborhood like this, before gunfire and sirens were the music of the street.

Chapman raised four children here on her own, one of whom, a boy, was murdered when he accompanied a friend on a drug deal gone sour. So many of the young men of the 'hood have died in violence that it is no longer a single reportable statistic, but a sadness that overlays the black ghetto like a mist of grief. Those who survive either leave the ghetto, become gang members, or spend the remainder of their lives ducking both bullets and the necessity to join their bros in running the subculture that thrives in their communities.

Chapman remains in the ghetto out of a moral commitment to make it better, working with children in a community project to keep them out of gangs and away from drugs. When the rioters of '92 burned and ravaged around her, she stayed behind locked doors . . . until she heard young thugs across the street trying to break into an auto supply place owned for many years by a Japanese family.

Disregarding her own safety, Chapman ran the hundred yards to the entryway of the building, stood in the doorway and ordered the toughs to spare the business. It was owned by good people, she said, who had contributed to the community and didn't deserve to see their lifelong enterprise perish. It was her courage and her commanding presence, not her logic, that kept the building whole for the moment. The young men left, humbled by her defiance, but others returned in the night, looted the business, then burned it to the ground. The lot stands empty today.

It is 6:45 when I arrive at Chapman's house. Trulysia is snuggled down on a couch with a cloth doll. Chapman has been up since five, waiting. The streets of South Central are empty, both because of the earliness of the hour and because of the news about to break on radio and television. Chapman had watched TV since she awakened, not wanting to miss news of the verdict if it came earlier. The night before, a carload of young men had passed her small house, their fists thrust from the vehicle's window, shouting, "Not guilty, not guilty," as though to stir South Central into a calamity it obviously didn't want.

Now as time moves at a snail's crawl toward seven, she busies herself making coffee and heating sweet rolls. I watch an anchor team on television busy themselves with vacuity, because now, minutes before the verdict, there is nothing to do and nothing to talk about until the snail, setting its own pace, achieves its destination. "Everyone," an anchorman says, "is looking at seven o'clock. . . ."

The house is small and the living room dark, removed from the windows by a passageway leading to the front door, like a closed-in porch. Bars are on the windows. We drink coffee and make small talk to divert our attention from the ticking clock. No one touches the sweet rolls. Chapman talks about the detective who broke the news to her that her son was dead. They have become friends since, and he checks on her often. "He's a rare kind of human being," she says.

And then it happens: 7 A.M.

The television scene switches to the Federal Court House. A reporter says, with understated irony, "Here comes the judge." Judge John Davies takes his place and calls for the verdict—*The Verdict*. Chapman stares at the set, transfixed. Trulysia sits up, clutching the cloth doll. At nine, she is totally aware of what's going on. Far off, a siren sounds. Chapman glances toward the direction of the sound but says nothing. The flashing presence of a new concern disappears almost instantly as she reconcentrates on the television screen.

The chairman of the jury is standing. He reads the verdicts: Stacey

Koon, guilty. Lawrence Powell, guilty. Timothy Wind, not guilty. Theodore Briseno, not guilty.

With each verdict of guilty, Chapman says, *"Yes!"* With each verdict of acquittal, she remains silent. Trulysia listens and then sinks back on the couch. "Justice has been done," Chapman says. "Tomorrow we'll have a barbecue." She telephoned neighbors and relatives. Most are elated that at least the two worst cops have been found guilty. Others insist all of them should go to jail. There will be speculation later that the jury had reached a "community verdict," i.e., a decision that would make everyone relatively happy and upset no one enough to cause the city to burn again.

It doesn't matter. The great fear that all four of the cops would go free is allayed with the two convictions. The threat of a new riot is over. South Central will go back to what it was before, mostly ignored, impoverished, often violent, and always a shadow on the edge of the city's conscience. But there is a new caring, and if the organization called Rebuild L.A., sprang from the '92 riots, seems inadequate, at least its ghost continues to haunt and to whisper its message to those still open enough to listen . . . to those who remember.

The visiting press? Those hungry armies of reporters that came to chronicle the verdict and a new riot? They leave almost disappointed that L.A. hasn't burned again, and in their disappointment toss parting shots at the city in Southern California that somehow manages to remain whole amid multicultural strife. The *Washington Post* says we are "economically shattered." The *San Francisco Chronicle* says we are "the reigning symbol of America's urban decay." *Business Week* says we are "wracked by crime, unemployment, and racial strife." The *Chicago Tribune* says we are "a stressed-out city, armed to the teeth, looking for a reason to believe in itself."

Shortcut Bernstein looks at me later that day, as we are having a drink at a bar in the Valley called Pineapple Hill, and says, "We're just a little tired." I think that's it.

 SEVEN

*I'm taking lessons in learning how to wave
to the poor.*
—Dick Riordan, fun-loving millionaire
mayor of Los Angeles

He seems like a friendly fellow.
—A poor man who waves back

WHEN THE RACE for mayor of Los Angeles came down to the wire in the spring of '93, Michael Woo thought he had it knocked. While polls showed him barely even with millionaire Dick Riordan, something wonderful happened only days from the election that brightened his life. There was a sudden revelation that Riordan, who up until then was Mr. Straight, had been arrested three times for drunk driving. Everyone figured in car-conscious L.A. that that kind of bombshell would be the edge that would make Woo mayor, the kiss a toad awaits on his way to becoming a prince. It was even better than the tepid endorsement he had received earlier from Bill Clinton, and better than the widespread rumor that his headquarters had been visited by the ghost of Elvis Presley.

Woo jumped on the arrests like a dog in heat and mentioned them at every opportunity in the kind of admonishing tone reserved for naughty children and demented uncles. What made it worse for Riordan was that at first he only admitted to two of the arrests. Then, afraid somebody would find out, he revealed, well, he'd forgotten a third one. This prompted a joyful Woo to respond that the guy wasn't only a drunk, but a dishonest drunk. Could you trust a schmuck like that to be mayor?

Well . . . yes.

The reason we could trust a schmuck like that to be mayor is that they were both schmucks, and it was just a case of which was the lesser of them. For all of his pious posturing, Woo was a prissy lightweight who, as a city councilman, couldn't even clean up his own corner of town. I pointed out in a column that he had made Hollywood safe for women and little children all right, as he had so frequently claimed, but only if they were hookers or dealers. All others remained in peril.

Riordan, on the other hand, maintained that he was tough enough to turn L.A. around from the general erosion it has been suffering the past several years, and the fact that he could have a few belts while doing it gave him a kind of John Wayne persona that was hard for L.A.'s middle class to resist. The Duke is a saint in this town, and anyone big enough to fill his boots is welcome to belly up to the bar with the rest of us.

Riordan's second-biggest campaign gambit was a boast that, as a venture capitalist, his massive infusion of cash had saved the Mattel Toy Company from going into the toilet, implying, I suppose, that he might do the same for L.A. The Mattel venture occurred during the big-spending '80s, when Riordan managed to amass an estimated $74 million in personal profit through eight large corporate deals, seven of which were leveraged buyouts.

When Woo tried to portray him as a drooling, money-grubbing ogre who cared nothing about the poor, Riordan replied that he was a capitalist with a heart and had created hundreds of jobs by saving companies rather than destroying them. An *L.A. Times* story revealed that while making himself a fortune, he had managed a net gain of only fourteen jobs, but that went unnoticed in the wash of political rhetoric. So did the comment made by Riordan to a journalist in 1981, at the height of his moneymaking: "I'm taking lessons in learning how to wave to the poor." Woo tried to make hay out of that, too, but the voters apparently concluded that by taking lessons in waving to the poor, Riordan had revealed his abiding interest and concern for the down and out, hoo-boy!

The campaign came to an end with a lot of nasty little spitting, most of it from Woo. Riordan came out of it looking pretty good, despite those drunk-driving arrests, or maybe because of them. His boast that he had saved a toy company for the children of America didn't hurt. While not exactly the parting of the Red Sea, it combined with the macho image to win him an 8 percent spread. Toys and booze are an odd combination with which historians will have to contend when they attempt to define the politics of '93, but that's their problem.

So now we have a schmuck running City Hall, which he bought for the $10 million he spent in the campaign, of which $2 million came from his own deep pockets. He's not the quickest guy on the block, and he's about as articulate as Donald Duck, but we're stuck with him. Now the question looms large over the town's beleaguered, pissed-upon, burned-out, shot-at, overburdened Angelenos: is *anyone* tough enough to turn L.A. around?

TRAVELIN' SAM YORTY was still mayor when I came to the Mother of All Whores, and God still lived in San Francisco. They called him Travelin' Sam because he spent as much time as possible seeing the world on city money, promoting, as it were, L.A. An amiable, pink-faced man, he loved Hollywood and the celebrities who traditionally cluster around City Hall. He could bullshit with the best of them and drink with the rest of them. Johnny Carson, who moved his show to L.A. a year before Yorty got booted from office, loved him. He was, in the grand tradition of big-city mayors, colorful, bombastic, outrageous, and . . . well . . . fun.

In fact, he is still fun at age eighty-five. I visited him one day in his large, tree-shaded house that was once owned by Mickey Rooney. Everyone who is anybody in L.A. lives in a house once owned by Somebody. I partied one night in a place where, it is said, Spencer Tracy made love to Katharine Hepburn. The owner insisted you could still hear the moans, and possibly some of the clever dialogue. Yorty's place sits on a hill overlooking the San Fernando Valley, like the estate of an aging baron living among his yesterdays. I had gone to see Mayor Sam to ask him what he thought about a debate raging in City Hall over ethics. By cutting his pay, the City Council had just lost its new ethics czar, and I wanted to know how Sam felt about an ethics czar in the first place, since his administration had been noticeably without one.

"An ethical person doesn't have to be told what ethics are," Yorty growled as he led me through his house, "and an unethical person can always find a way around them." He became mayor in 1961 and served a turbulent dozen years that included campus uprisings and the destructive Watts riots. A vigorous and creative campaigner, he had beaten Tom Bradley once in a contest with racist overtones, but couldn't best him in '73. It was a new L.A. back then, and Yorty belonged to the old one.

"I got these medals turning Los Angeles into a world city," Sam was saying as he led me from room to room in what he called his Rogue's Gallery. There was the Great Silver Insignia from Austria, the ornate Order of the Homayoun from "old Iran," the Finnish Lion from Finland, and the Order of the Sun from Peru. He was as bombastic as ever, though a little slower in getting out of a chair than he used to be when he was mayor and bounced up, hand extended, like a toy popped into the air by a spring.

"Ethics is just right or wrong," Sam said, getting back to the reason for my visit. "You don't need a damned commission to tell you that." He pointed to a photograph on the wall. "That's me with the Shah of Iran. Hell of a nice guy." Yorty with Jawaharlal Nehru, Yorty with Chiang Kai-shek, Yorty with Zsa Zsa Gabor. "Too many people run for office for the easy money. You don't know they're unethical until it's too late. Me with Golda Meir. A fine woman."

Yorty is proud of the fact that he was investigated for months by a team of reporters who came up empty-handed. "The most they could do was nail a harbor commissioner," he says, smiling slightly at the memory. "They didn't get a thing on Yorty. That's me with Princess Margaret. A damned sweet lady."

Kahlil Gibran said, "He who defines his conduct by ethics imprisons his songbird in a cage." Nobody ever accused Sam of imprisoning his songbird.

THE MAYORS OF Los Angeles have been an undistinguished lot who have faded into the background of history with very little impact on the present. That L.A. has survived their presence is a wonder in itself, since many in the past 140 years were nothing more than ritualistic caretakers of a city growing and expanding on its own. Other forces, such as the *L.A. by God Times,* ran City Hall off and on, while the mayor sat on his throne and smiled dimly. There wasn't even a Fiorello LaGuardia in their midst. No one read the funny papers over the radio. One doubted if some of them could even read.

There were crooks among them and charlatans. One mayor resigned to head a lynch mob. One hanged himself in the council chambers. One couldn't speak English. Alpheus P. Hodges set the standard. He was elected L.A.'s first mayor on July 1, 1850, several months before California was admitted into the union. At twenty-eight, he is still the youngest person ever to hold that office. His birthday isn't celebrated because no one knows when he was born. His photograph doesn't hang in City Hall because there isn't one. The second mayor of L.A., Benjamin Wilson, has a mountain named after him. Tom Bradley's name graces an airport terminal and a subway station. Nothing is named after Alpheus P. Hodges.

We know he was a leading physician in the town back in the days before cars, smog, Evian water, Chinese chicken salads, Michael Jackson, and open-mouthed kissing. L.A. was considered a pueblo then. That means town or village. Its 1,610 inhabitants lived in small, square adobes with flat roofs. U.S. troops still occupied the place when Alpheus was elected mayor. The narrow dirt streets were clouds of dust or seas of mud, depending on the weather.

Little is known of Hodges. He hailed from Virginia, but why he came to Southern California remains a mystery. There weren't any movie studios in those days and the gold veins were farther north, although serving simultaneously as coroner and mayor, Alpheus did get a hundred dollars each time he presided over the inquest of a dead Indian. History fails to record what he was paid for non-Indians. It does say, however, he was a drinking man and dabbled in real estate, becoming co-owner of the Bella Union Hotel. It was the County Courthouse until 1851.

Of his accomplishments, only one major undertaking is listed in a City Hall pamphlet. "It is said that under his vigorous administration, there was projected and carried to completion a wooden water ditch that remained long a monument to his intelligent enterprise." I think it's still there. The Alpheus P. Hodges Water Ditch. At last. A monument.

SAM YORTY WAS a lot more fun than that. Tom Bradley was, too. But just barely. Unfortunately for Yorty, L.A. was not in a fun mood in 1973, and Bradley—a sharecropper's son who was both an ex-cop and an ex-councilman—ran him down. Bradley was in stark contrast to the ebullient Yorty and gave off the impression that his silence might conceal thoughts of great wisdom that he ultimately might share with a city still smarting from the Watts riots. Forget that.

I covered the race back then, and it was apparent almost from the start that Bradley was not an eloquent man, nor did great passions bubble easily to the surface. In short, he had the personality of a trout. And yet there were moments when the quietness revealed strands of steel. I remember standing alone with him in a solitary moment on the city's Westside, where L.A.'s huge Jewish population was indicating its support with crowds far larger than anyone expected.

Bradley had just said, "People are listening this time. They're hearing what we have to say and they're not caring what color we are. There's no racial thing this time." Then there was the silence again as we stood together at the edge of the crowds, sharing the sudden gap in activity. That was when the steel showed through. Perhaps he was thinking of the racial overtones of the '69 race. Perhaps his dislike of Yorty was inexorably intertwined with a feeling of victimization. He said without preamble, without reason, "I began this campaign the moment I lost the last one. I've wanted Sam a long, long time."

He won with a coalition of blacks and Jews that was to be a hallmark of his administration. If nothing else, the election of one of the first black mayors in a major American city gave L.A. its first hint of a multiracial character. Women and minorities found their way into city government under Bradley, who encouraged their presence by his presence. His greatest moments, some say, were when the mayor simply stood and managed something of a smile and said nothing.

Bradley's encouragement of women and minorities into positions of prominence didn't always serve him well. One longtime associate, Juanita St. John, was accused of bilking a Los Angeles–African trade task force out of $180,000. The city, mostly at Bradley's behest, had given the task force nearly $400,000 during a four-year period. St. John headed the unit. She was also treasurer of Global Alert, an antigenocide group, from which she was accused of stealing $5,000. A jury deadlocked on the first charge (a new trial was pending), but convicted her of stealing from Global Alert. She was sentenced to ninety days in the county jail.

What made the scandal even more interesting is that for a time, Bradley and St. John were partners in a real estate venture that Bradley was lobbying the City Council to fund. And to finally warm the cozy relationship, Bradley hired St. John's daughter at City Hall, and St. John hired Bradley's daughter at the task force.

Bradley managed to slip out of that peccadillo by selling his interests in the real estate venture at the first hint of an investigation and by effectively distancing himself from St. John. We began calling him the Teflon mayor for his demonstrable ability to slide away from scandal; not just this one but other problems that struck at the heart of the moral purity he waved like a flag in his City Hall office. But the scandals overlapped and for the first time brought into question Bradley's ethical conduct as mayor.

The most serious arose with reports that Silent Tom had served as paid adviser to two financial institutions that had dealings with the city. One, in fact, Far East National Bank, received $2 million in city deposits the same day *(aha!)* that Bradley telephoned the city treasurer to ask about the bank's status, though, God knows, he had not (he insisted) tried to influence anybody about anything.

An investigation by the city attorney cleared the mayor of any legal wrongdoing but declared that he had become "indifferent to ethical concerns." Bradley apologized publicly with a clever *mea culpa* that acknowledged "errors in judgment" by creating the appearance that he was a crook when he wasn't. He returned $18,000 he had received from Far East after learning that the bank had received deposits from the city. But it wasn't over.

Questions arose about his use of undue influence to help business associates and about his stock portfolio. Once more, the city attorney filed action against the mayor, this time for failing to disclose personal investments worth $160,000. Bradley agreed to pay a $20,000 fine to settle the matter, and again managed to slip off the griddle with the skill of the professional he had become. Other investigations settled slowly over the horizon and disappeared.

Bradley would call that year of scandals, 1989, the worst year of his life, but who did he end up blaming? The media, of course. "Maybe somebody's trying to win a Pulitzer by being another Woodward and Bernstein," he said, in reference to the two *Washington Post* reporters who broke the Watergate scandal. Only the press seemed to concern itself with the ethical questions circling like buzzards over City Hall; the people couldn't have cared less. "They don't understand what the whole thing was all about," the mayor said. But, still . . . polls showed his popularity lower than it had ever been. But what the hell. Whadda they know?

That Bradley was resilient, no one ever doubted. Twice he ran for governor of California and twice was defeated, once by the narrowest of margins, but he somehow managed to weather the disappointments with characteristic stoicism. His was not an easy five terms of office. The years paralleled my own, and together we have weathered earthquakes, storms, gang wars, wildfires, drought, recession, and riots. We have seen L.A. change from a reasonably safe city to an often dangerous one, with guns as popular as eye twicks and butt tucks. Nobody walks at night anymore, except in malls patrolled by cops. They're like refugee camps. It's safe inside where the cops are, but don't trust the shadows at the edge of the light.

On the plus side of his stewardship, Bradley's L.A. boasts a revitalized downtown, a larger and more efficient international airport, a harbor that's now number one in the nation, an energized program of arts and culture, cleaner air and water, and the beginning of a new electric transit system that's about fifty years too late. He scoffed at those who said the 1984 Olympics would be a money-losing venture beset by domestic gangs and international terrorists, and points to the fact that the games were among the most lucrative and successful in the history of the Olympics.

But mostly he crows about bringing the diverse cultural elements of the city together by making them a part of City Hall. He told a gathering on the day he announced that he would not seek a sixth term: "When I first entered office, I saw only a tiny part of our diverse community represented in the halls of government. I am proud to say I changed that. We took a city that belonged to one group and gave it to all the people."

THERE WERE FIFTY-TWO candidates for mayor at the outset of the 1993 election. One was a twenty-two-year-old musician who voted for Goofy in the prior Presidential election, one had been recently arrested for screaming and waving a Cajun-fried fish in public, one campaigned on a platform of ending hysterectomies, and one wanted to blow the smog out of L.A. with giant fans.

There were singers among them and street-corner dancers and unemployed actors and plumbers and homeless people and people who had been told by God to run, although God later denied telling anyone anything. Mayoral candidates were of all shapes, sizes, colors, and ages, and included at least four of L.A.'s many and varied sexes. Political analysts dismissed them as clutter. Shortcut Bernstein was not so sure. "Dead guys have won elections in the past," he said.

"Why not a naked Lithuanian midget who dances on street corners to Madonna tapes played on a ghetto blaster?"

Candidates for mayor are required to either gather the signatures of a thousand registered voters or pay three hundred dollars and gather five hundred signatures. Those unwilling or unable to do either quickly vanished from sight in the contest. That left twenty-four candidates in the primary, twenty-two of whom were eliminated by the time we got to the general election. That left only Woo, Riordan, Bob Hope, Clint Eastwood, Danny DeVito, and Charlton Heston. As Desi Arnaz used to say, let me 'splain.

In Los Angeles, no public project is ever undertaken and no election ever held without a celebrity endorsement. Most of them do it for big bucks, such as those who endorse commercial products, some do it for what they perceive to be flashes of principle, and others do it in order to keep their name before the public. I do not know the motives of those who announced their backing of either Riordan or Woo, so we must assume that their enthusiasm sprang from a well of political commitment of which we were not previously aware.

Riordan's celebrity endorsers included the old-timers: Bob Hope, Clint Eastwood, Charlton Heston, and Ronald Reagan, an actor who used to be in politics, too. Woo's celebrities included Oliver Stone, who solved the assassination of John Kennedy, the brothers Lloyd and Jeff Bridges, Ted Danson, Danny DeVito, and Bill Clinton, who is currently in politics but striving to be a Hollywood celebrity.

The endorsements of Hope, Heston, and Reagan were dismissable. Hope couldn't even gather a crowd at a fund-raiser some weeks earlier, Heston had been reduced to doing commercials for William Buckley's National Review, and Reagan just didn't count anymore. Similarly forgettable were the Woo endorsements by Stone, who had become a parody of himself, the brothers Bridges (nice guys, but so what?), Danson, a blackface comic, and Clinton, who said he liked Woo but Riordan seemed good too and he was certainly willing to back Woo but he could work with Riordan and . . . well, you get the idea. When Riordan won, he visited Washington and they went jogging together.

That left Eastwood, who had just won an Oscar for *Unforgiven,* and DeVito, who does everything well. Riordan and Woo, by their very nature, were not enchanting personalities. If you looked at them long enough, they seemed to blur into one figure, a kind of Chinese Irishman with money. But their alter egos, Eastwood and DeVito, were both special people, which made it difficult to chose between them. True, Eastwood was taller, but DeVito had a sort of puckish energy that lit the screen.

"The trouble with both of them," Shortcut Bernstein said, "is that neither of them is young and sexy. Also, neither is a woman. This is the year of the woman. If Sharon Stone were running, every flash of her crotch would mean at least five percentage points." He was referring to the movie *Basic Instinct* in which Stone flashes a group of policemen, including the main protagonist, Michael Douglas.

"There was a rumor it wasn't her crotch," I said to Shortcut.

"It was her crotch," he said firmly. "It was a full-body shot. They couldn't have superimposed someone else's crotch between her legs."

"That's not what I mean. Remember when they used to use pasties over women's nipples because blue laws wouldn't allow them to show the actual nipple?"

"I guess so."

"Well," I said, "rumor has it that it was a false crotch made of some exotic, lifelike material, glued, or however they affix it, over Stone's crotch."

"I'll be damned," Shortcut said, shaking his head. "It's amazing what they can do with plastics these days."

"That's just a rumor," I said. "To the best of my knowledge, no one has ever asked her if it was her crotch or an ersatz crotch."

"I guess we'll never know," Shortcut said, somewhat wistfully.

"I guess."

Neither Eastwood nor DeVito revealed their crotches during the campaign; likewise, Riordan and Woo. Therefore, it was left to the voters to pick the personality they liked best, since nothing else matters in L.A. We are, after all, the place that gave you Ronald Reagan, Richard Nixon, and George Murphy.

As it turned out, we liked Eastwood better because, I think, he's taller and rangier. I would have voted for Sharon Stone. Greatness is founded on lesser qualities than a nice crotch.

EIGHT

*Los Angeles is a city no worse than others, a
city rich and vigorous and full of pride, a
city lost and beaten and full of emptiness.*
—Raymond Chandler

I SAW A naked fat lady in Los Angeles one day. She was striding de-
terminedly across an overpass that spans the Hollywood Freeway just
north of downtown. She carried her clothes under one arm and was
heading in a straight line toward the Civic Center, with a mission in
mind that required full concentration. She looked neither to the left
nor to the right, but straight ahead, ignoring the signals that controlled heavy traffic on a frontage road leading toward Broadway,
somehow managing to miss being run over.

It was a busy time of day and hundreds must have seen her. Cars
and pedestrians passed by her without much notice, except for the
drivers forced to slam on their brakes to avoid hitting her. They
cursed and shouted and shook their fists in rage, willing to accept
her total nudity as none of their business, but unwilling to allow anyone, naked or not, to violate their right-of-way during the commute
hour.

I followed her for several blocks and was amazed at what little attention she earned. Even a cop parked just off Broadway paid scant
notice as she strode by him. When I asked didn't he see the naked
woman walking down Broadway he said, yes, she's been reported
and would be picked up and taken to the psycho ward at County
Hospital. Then he went back to the report he was writing. I went

off to work, wondering about the awful absurdity of the situation. The naked fat lady becomes a metaphor for Los Angeles. We are a naked city, vulnerable as hell, striding with great determination toward a destination that remains a mystery not only to most of the rest of the world, but to many of us who live here and attempt to understand the place. If there were a psycho ward for cities, we would be there undergoing intensive treatment for a character disorder, with a 40 percent chance for full recovery. That isn't much, but it's better than New York.

URBAN SELF-ANALYSIS sprang from the ashes of the riots. After the fires died, we blamed ourselves for the mess and spent a year wringing our hands and sobbing, "Hit me," like so many civic sadomasochists looking for a little pain. It was especially hard on white liberals from Malibu and Beverly Hills who assumed personal responsibility for not having, well, cared more. They knelt all over the city for weeks, sobbing and banging their heads on the pavement.

You'd think that after all that anguish we'd come up with some stable course of action to make things better between the races generally and in the South-Central section particularly. But what emerged wasn't a powerful program to enfranchise the forgotten, but a call, you guessed it, to improve our image. Keep the naked fat lady who in her madness strides nowhere, but tie a nice little ribbon in her hair.

The first post-riot effort to put a sheen on our tarnished image was a suggestion that we initiate an "I Love L.A." campaign, a little red heart substituting for the word love. Use of the phrase, you might recall, is not new. We are not a place big on originality, despite our prominence as entertainment capital of the world. What we've added to film and television is sex, and sex was only popularized, not invented, in Hollywood. Even dinosaurs were doing it . . . though, as it turned out, probably not all that well.

New York was the first major city to utilize the "I Love" campaign and the little red heart. "I ♥ NY" was everybody's bumper sticker for years, after which the Big Apple became a place of peace and love and hardly any crime or violence at all. Thereafter, Americans fell in love with their towns from coast to coast and eventually around the world, flaunting bumper stickers in many languages, like flags of urban passion. Only places like Oakland, to the best of my knowledge, remained unloved, though inhabited. "I Tolerate Oakland" might have worked, but no one suggested it.

The L.A. campaign was initiated by the L.A. Convention and Visitors Bureau, following an offer by a Pittsburgh public relations man to design the whole enchilada. It would have cost $30 million a year, which the Visitors Bureau promised to raise through private contributions. The campaign was praised by the City Council after one of its members suggested there was too damned much negativity about Los Angeles in both the local and national media. The member's name is Laura Chick, who represents the San Fernando Valley. That is not a name I made up, or one that she made up, for that matter. Thank God, we don't have a John Dude on the council. How would we ever live it down? Chick was tired of the media's downgrading of the city she loves, and brought the matter to the attention of the full council, whose other members mumbled their agreement.

What irked Chick to the max, as they say around the malls, was a segment on CBS's *48 Hours* that asked, "Has L.A.'s moment in the sun passed?" A few months earlier, *Time* magazine wondered in a cover story, "Is the City of Angels Going to Hell?" *Newsweek,* not to be outdone, similarly defined our downfall in a piece called "Looking Past the Verdict," meaning, at that time, the Rodney King verdict. By the way, the "I ♥ NY" campaign followed a *Time* cover piece that asked no questions. It just said, "The Rotting of the Big Apple."

I tried to counter our own negativity with a Think Good Thoughts About L.A. campaign, but, unfortunately, it came out wrong. I wanted a bumper sticker to say "Welcome to L.A., Take Cover." I was, therefore, one of the local media people Chick wanted to overcome. Her campaign began with a thundering volley before the City Council. She stood right up and said, "We're doing incredibly wonderful things in L.A.!" Way to go, Chick.

Unfortunately, however, that campaign came acropper when it was revealed that a mainstay of the effort would have been billboards that, for a reason no one quite understood, would have listed the city's bad points along with its wonderfulness. One billboard, for instance, would have been composed of L.A.'s "teams": the Dodgers, the Lakers, and the Kings on one side and, on the other, the Crips, Bloods, and V13, which are among our more active gangs. Splashed across the bottom would have been the logo: "L.A.: It's all how you look at it."

I'm not sure what went on in the mayor's office when the campaign was unveiled, whether they threw up, killed and buried the creator of the billboard idea, or just cried like babies, but the whole thing was thrown out like so much kitchen garbage and never mentioned again. The only city response came from a mayor's aide, who said coolly, "It was not a good idea."

What followed was the creation of the New Los Angeles Marketing Partnership, or New LAMP, to sing the praises of L.A. and its environs in an advertising campaign that will last for five years. New LAMP hired the agency that celebrated eggs in television commercials depicting them marching out of prison and the slogan "Eggs, give them a break." One of the owners of the agency, Brad Ball, admitted that L.A. would be a tough sell due to all off the disasters that had rained on us like pigeon shit, but added that it would be an exciting challenge "because this is definitely a glass half-full and not a glass half-empty situation."

Our new slogan will be "Together we're the best, Los Angeles!" The exclamation point is theirs.

IT ALL HAS to do with tourism. We get about 20 million visitors each summer. They come from Japan, England, New York (though reluctantly), Botswana, Dallas, Denver, and Pottawatomie, Kansas. Each spends an average of $39.50 a day, and while it is difficult accepting cash from anyone dressed in red shorts and a Hawaiian shirt, we still manage to do so. They don't know about *haute couture* in Pottawatomie. They're not even trying to be grunge-hip. Comfort is everything in the heartland.

Tourism is our second-biggest industry in L.A. Five hundred million dollars was spent to expand our convention center. If the conventioneers don't come, the center will rot and decay and become another Roman Colosseum. *Then* maybe the tourists will flock to the City of Angles, the way they go to Rome, to look at the ruins.

The thinking here is if we don't clean up our act, nobody's going to flock here, despite all the wonderful things that Laura Chick perceives. Those who have come this far in the book know that realities in L.A. are harsh: kids with guns shoot each other on the streets and in the schools. Punks devoid of compassion and without the ability to measure consequences drive our streets armed to the teeth. A word or look can invite disaster. The territorial imperative is a bloody line drawn across the face of the city.

Things were so bad at the start of 1993 that a group associated with the Maharishi Mahesh Yogi offered to save L.A. through Transcendental Meditation. It would cost the city only $165 million a year for five years. That would finance nine thousand "coherence-creating experts" who would seek deeper levels of consciousness through TM and radiate peace and goodwill into the troubled areas of the county, which is just about everywhere except the gated communities that hire guards and snarling dogs. A press agent for the group explained that it takes a thousand experts per million population to work. Forget the cost, the press agent said. L.A. would get it back in the money spent by the coherence experts through hotel bills, meals, transportation, and souvenirs, especially those sequined puce-toned hats with HOLLYWOOD scrawled across the front.

I was so intrigued by the notion that I arranged to talk by telephone to the Maharishi himself, who was at his headquarters in Amsterdam. Anyone over forty probably remembers him from the 1960s. He was a monk in India prior to then, but in the sixties founded Transcendental Meditation and became an international figure. TM sprang to prominence because it involved only thinking. You didn't have to actually *do* anything, a situation which many found pleasantly relaxing. The Maharishi, given generally good press, became a guru to the Beatles, among other luminaries. That may not mean much now, but it impressed the hell out of us in the '60s. But then, so did psychedelic tattoos and flowered tiaras.

I found the Maharashi to be a generally good-natured man who insisted the idea was not to make a profit but to save Los Angeles. "You must not think we are making money," he said in a tonal quality that managed to be both reedy and lyrical. He sounded a little like an East Indian impersonation of himself.

The nine thousand coherence experts would be necessary to stir the proper vibrations. They're trained to create a powerful influence of harmony, balance and positivity in the atmosphere, and thereby neutralize criminal tendencies. The mind goes deep into itself, quieting to a silent state through the mental repetition of a word or phrase. The phrase is in Sanskrit. Minds thus free of stress create a chain reaction of peace in society. It's so long drive-bys, hello love.

"It's simple," the Maharishi said.

"If it's so simple," I said, "why can't we do it and save $165 million a year?"

"It takes training," he added quickly.

"Would it be correct to say it's only a matter of thinking good thoughts?"

"No," he said somewhat testily. I could hear voices in the background, advisers telling him to lighten up. "It creates a positive influence that spreads," he finally said in a more pleasant tone. "It worked in Iowa."

I asked then-Mayor Tom Bradley if he was prepared to spend $165 million a year for five years to eliminate crime in L.A. He said if he had $165 million to spend he'd use it to hire more cops. *Click.* We just weren't ready for cosmic love.

IF THERE IS one thing we are aware of in L.A. it's tourism. Despite our current reputation as Hell City, visitors continue to come from all over the world. In 1987, when gunfire briefly replaced the middle finger as a means of communicating displeasure on our freeways, tourists seemed to look upon it as a kind of ride on a Disneyland conveyance, where one of those funny little cars sweeps by an automatic dispenser that fires blanks at them as they dip and whiz out of the way, their occupants screaming with fright and joy.

Humans are naturally drawn to chaos. They are also drawn to mass recreational events, which is why Michael Jackson and Pope John Paul II have always done so well when they have appeared on the great stages of the world. Permanent areas of recreational activity also attract crowds, such as Disneyland, Universal Studios, Knott's Berry Farm, and Six Flags Magic Mountain, where one can simultaneously enjoy the attractions offered and possibly see a gang member, although they are kept out if recognized. Sometimes, though, you can't tell a gang member from a Malibu teenager who is trying to look like a gang member. Gangbanger chic, i.e., baggy clothes, a bandanna, and a Dodgers hat worn backward, is the preferred mode of fashion in the grungy pubescent set.

In addition to the usual attractions that lure tourists by the millions to L.A., there are also the sporadic attractions, such as the freeway shootings and even the riots of '92, as I mentioned earlier. This year it's the O.J. Simpson double-murder trial, which, among the sobering moments of blood-sampling and cop-trashing, has also featured a man in drag thrown out of court for arguing loudly with another spectator, defense attorneys who, like petulant starlets, weren't speaking to each other, and a small plane overhead trailing a banner that complimented prosecutor Marcia Clark on her new hairdo. The not-guilty verdict reached by a jury that wouldn't have known DNA from the PTA added a final level of surreality to the proceedings. The decision to free O.J. was achieved in less time than it takes to complete Monday-night football and left many of us pondering in despair the troubling posture of justice that fame and money can create.

But before all that there was Heidi Fleiss, whose crime involved sex rather than violence, but whose audience was equally attentive.

She was the twenty-seven-year-old pediatrician's daughter who allegedly ran a stable of beautiful young women whom she, well, rented out to movie stars, directors, producers, agents, million-dollar film writers, and others in The Industry able to afford $1,000 or $1,500 for a night to remember.

They called her saga the Heidi Chronicles and Heidi herself the Madam to the Stars. She was compared to Sydney Biddle Barrows, the so-called Mayflower Madam, an uppercrust descendent of the Pilgrims whose high-class New York call girl ring was busted up in 1984. Heidi couldn't trace her roots back to Plymouth Rock, but she certainly added glamour to a profession that can be traced back to the Greeks but probably flourished before that in a more primitive form.

What was so attractive about the Heidi Chronicles was that it involved the big players in Hollywood. We were all certain that Heidi's Big Black Gucci Book contained the names of her customers, and, like kids peeking in the bedroom, we were dying to get a look at it. Rumors circulated. Two male celebrities stepped forward to deny they were among Heidi's clients even though no names had been released. There was speculation that they were doing it for status, that they had never been Heidi's customers but wanted to be counted among the big spenders who actually were. A standup comic I know is offering $1,500 to get his name *in* the black book. Th-th-that's Hollywood, folks.

The existence of a Madam to the Stars doesn't surprise me. I know of a Bailbondsman to the Stars, a Roofer to the Stars, a Milkman to the Stars, a Carwasher to the Stars, a Yogi to the Stars, and even an Oracle to the Stars, so why not a procurer who caters to the same sort of celebrity clientele? Not every high roller has his own groupies. Sometimes you have to send out for them, the way an average guy sends out for pepperoni pizza.

At any rate, those brief, brilliant news bytes out of L.A. that circle the world like whiffs of a whore's cologne are what keeps the tourists interested. Not that they had a chance in hell of seeing Heidi. She became reclusive under the intensity of media scrutiny. But they might have caught a glimpse of a Heidigirl if they dropped by one of the hot restaurants or bars that seemed to attract them. The only problem was, by the time they got there the hot restaurant or bar might have been out of business, unable to maintain the heat that the brief attention spans of hookers or celebs required. What's hot today may not be hot tomorrow, so transitory is the nature of fame in a city that eats its young.

Tourists feast on L.A.'s flashes of sexual notoriety. The Heidi story was still bubbling when Cinelli and I returned from a trip through Europe. We had driven three thousand miles through Northern Italy, France, and Spain in an effort to trace the roots of our heritage. The trip had been suggested years ago by my good friend Alex Haley, who thought I was Portuguese. He said I should go to Lisbon, which he considered a glorious city. When someone told him I was Mexican, he couldn't believe it. I clarified that by telling him I was only Mexican when it suited my purpose, being a columnist in a place with a large Mexican population. Actually, I am mostly Basque. Cinelli is mostly Italian. That's why we went to mostly Spain and Northern Italy. Alex said we should go to Lisbon anyhow, but we didn't.

We had watched some of the Heidi Chronicles on CNN and were aware it was the Story of the Summer, not only in L.A. but throughout the world. I decided we would be tourists in Los Angeles upon our return in order to see the city through the eyes of visitors. It was a good coming-home column anyhow. Writing a column again after a long absence is like trying to have a baby in your fifties. It's possible but not easy. Seeing Heidi-Era L.A. as a tourist was a viable concept. So we went from the airport to a nearby hotel and signed up for a four-hour tour.

Our tour bus driver was from Brooklyn, so we got a lot of dats and deres over the PA system, such as, "Youse folks would be interested in dat dere place over on da left. . . ." The most vocal passenger was a Born Again Christian Okie. He reminded me of a preacher I once interviewed in Wichita, Kansas. I was writing a piece on what others thought of L.A. He said, "The mountains between Wichita and Los Angeles are strewn with the pages of the Bible that are thrown from the windows of airplanes by those going to that Godless place."

The Okie on the tour bus felt the same way. When the bus driver mentioned Heidi as we drove through Hollywood, the Okie shouted that she was proof God had abandoned Los Angeles. "God walks out," he said loudly, "when whores walk in." A couple from Oslo laughed at him, which only made the Okie more vocal. The bus driver and most of the others aboard ignored him. A group of Japanese took notes. They are a peculiar race. Cinelli thinks it's because they're crowded together on those little islands. "That's why bees get so crazy," she said, "crammed together in tiny hives."

We drove through Beverly Hills and Bel-Air and their environs. Spike da tour bus driver pointed out the homes of stars. Of special interest to him was Eddie Murphy's home. "I'll bet he's got himself some nice little groupies," Spike said. One imagined drool at the corners of his mouth. "God will deal with him in His own good time," the Okie said, nodding knowingly. "Dat's where Michael J. Fox used to live," the bus driver said. I had pizza once with Fox when I was writing a profile of him for *TV Guide*. It was in his early years, when he was still cute.

In Hollywood, we stopped to watch Billy Graham get his own star on the Walk of Fame, near what used to be Grauman's Chinese Theater, now Mann's Chinese Theater. Everybody gets a star now. A Japanese tourist wanted to know who Billy Graham was. "A Christian," the Okie replied smartly. "Ahhh," the tourist said, writing it down.

The couple from Oslo wanted Spike to take them to a Heidi bar, but Spike said it wasn't included in the tour. Ditto the area of the riots. Now tourists ask about where Nicole Brown Simpson and Ron Goldman were murdered, and where O.J. lived. "You have to get a private driver for dat," Spike said to the couple who asked about the Heidi bar. "Maybe a taxi or somethin'." We wandered out of Hollywood into the lackluster 'hoods that compose much of the Westside: Culver City, where MGM once reigned supreme, and the Fairfax District, where, as someone pointed out, we keep all the Jews. We keep CBS there, too.

The tour ended back at the hotel. For dinner, Cinelli and I chose a restaurant listed in the tour guide. It was a neo-Mexican place called Rebecca's. We sat under a giant red-domed octopus made of plastic beads and bathed in light. Its tentacles were amber and gold. It clung upside down to the ceiling like some magical, psychedelic spider.

Cinelli looked up at it and sighed. "Order a martini," she said. "We're home at last."

AND THE FAT lady disappeared down Spring Street.

NINE

THE ONLY CELEBRITIES I had seen in person before moving to L.A. were Chill Wills and Ted Kennedy. Even then, I didn't actually *see* Chill Wills, although his Cadillac with steer horns on the hood was parked in front of the Oakland Tribune Tower, a gothic brick edifice that stands empty today. One of my colleagues at the *Trib*, the hard-drinking Jerry Belcher, who later moved to the *L.A. Times*, where he died of sobriety and boredom, told me he had witnessed Chill Wills talking to our then publisher, the late William Fife Knowland. Wills was a sidekick cowboy actor of little consequence who was no doubt admired by the dull, right-wing Knowland, a former U.S. Senator, as a Great American. I can't think of another reason why he'd have been there.

I asked Belcher if he was absolutely certain it was Chill Wills, because in addition to drinking heavily much of the time, Belch was also subject to hallucinations, for which he was under medication. Once he thought he saw Ed McMahon emerge from his television set and wander through the living room. It was an experience he mentioned in revulsion, because he never cared for McMahon. I often drank with him (Belcher, not McMahon; I never saw him), although I didn't have his capacity for booze. I recall vaguely that we drank five martinis each for lunch one wintry day in 1957, and when I woke up it was 1962.

Old-timers still talk about the Time Chill Wills Came to Oakland, though hardly anyone remembers when Ted Kennedy swung by. It was in 1968, when Bobby was running for the Presidency, just before he went to L.A. and got murdered. I'm not sure why Teddy visited the *Trib* except to use the men's room. That's where I met him. We urinated side by side and, as men will, I stole a glance. I can tell you now why Teddy got such a reputation as a womanizer. It wasn't his fault; it was an anatomical anomaly that triggered his quest. No man was better endowed. He was simply following his star, the way Joe Montana pursued quarterbacking when he discovered his great throwing arm.

I said to Teddy, "How you doing, Senator," and he replied, "Fine, just fine," in that tone of voice Senators use on constituents, no matter what they're doing when the constituent approaches. Then he shook his dork a little, washed his hands, and was gone. I mention washing his hands because a fellow reporter, Bob Heisey, took a poll once and discovered that seven out of ten men do not, I repeat, do not wash their hands after using the bathroom. I don't know what else Heisey ever did, but that was important. One man he knew washed his hands *before* urinating, which is the height of either caution or ego.

The point is, those were the only two celebrities I ever saw in sixteen years of working for the *Oakland Tribune*. Someone said Frank Sinatra flew over once in his private plane en route to San Jose, but that could never be verified. That is one of the big differences between Oakland and L.A., although in many other respects they are similar. Celebrities are everywhere in L.A. They are practically jumping up and down in the middle of the street shouting, "Look at me, look at me!"

There are several different levels of fame or celebrityhood in the City of Angles. There is Fringe Fame, New Fame, Passing Fame, and Vintage Fame, plus some others I will mention as we progress. You don't have to be a film or television star to achieve celebrity status, although it helps. It also helps if you display your crotch on the big screen (Vaginal Fame), although it is not always necessary. Sharon Stone showed it all and for a while was on the cover of every major magazine in the country, from *Vanity Fair* to *Architectural Digest*. She did the talk show circuit. Asked by one interviewer why she revealed her womanhood, as he put it so blatantly, she replied, "It's my job."

Zsa Zsa Gabor is a good example of Fringe Fame. Remarkably devoid of even minimal talent, she has nonetheless managed to achieve some degree of notoriety by talking a lot and marrying frequently. Milton Berle (Vintage Fame) called her the Queen of Pussy at a Friar's Club roast, among other names, and she didn't seem to object. This was after she was found guilty of slapping a Beverly Hills policeman who had stopped her for a traffic violation. Crime Fame, by the way, is another method of achieving celebrityhood, which applies here. Zsa Zsa's trial was jammed with media coverage, and she loved it. More on Crime Fame (also Trial Fame and/or Passing Fame) later.

Roseanne represents New Fame, Passing Fame, and Vulgar Fame. The last category applies to the moment when she grabbed her crotch while singing America's National Anthem at the opening of a baseball All-Star Game. I don't mean to concentrate on public female genitalia in this section of the book, but that's just the way it is in L.A. We think about it a lot. That's why L.A. is called the Mother of Whores. Roseanne and her husband, now her ex-husband, managed to be in the news frequently by getting divorced, cursing critics, or leaving obscene notes for anyone foolish enough to park in their space at the ABC lot. While her show remains somehow popular, I am hoping it too will pass, which is why I placed her in the Passing Fame category.

So many others would be included in New Fame that it is impossible to mention them all; for instance, the entire cast of *Melrose Place*, who, God willing, will soon share a place in the annals of Passing Fame. Vintage Fame belongs to those who have somehow managed to endure as celebrities while growing old before our very eyes. You stare at a middle-aged woman trying to remember where you've seen her before and realize later that she was once Debbie Reynolds, the dancing darling of the 1950s, who lost Eddie Fisher to Liz Taylor at a time so long ago it was barely a part of the Cenozoic Era. Liz, by the way, would be in the category of Legendary Fame.

Attorney Gloria Allred, our Queen Feminist, is an example of those who achieve fame without being in show biz, although recently she was hired by a local television station to comment on passing events, regardless of their importance to the public weal, and by a radio station to run a talk show. That's peripheral show biz, I guess, if you play it right. She dresses in red occasionally, as befits her name, so as not to go unnoticed.

Allred's claim to fame has always been her ability to summon the media in a manner not unlike the Pied Piper of Hamelina, who tottled his flute to gather rats. Her cases have often been a little offbeat, which is why we are all so eager to attend her media shows. One involved a girl who was kicked off a high school cheerleading squad because her breasts were too large, and another a woman thrown out of a pricey Beverly Hills restaurant for breast-feeding her baby.

Due to Allred's trailblazing efforts, it is now all right to have large breasts if you're a cheerleader and it is permissible to breast-feed your baby in many of Beverly Hills' better eateries, though we'd prefer you didn't. Get a wet nurse or something and leave the baby home.

FAME HAS ITS PRICE, even if it is only fame by association that lasts for a few weeks. A prime example of that social hypothesis is the short, happy fling of David Bojorquez. David looked like any other aspiring actor in town, with the kind of open good looks that instill confidence. If he told you he worked for Steven Spielberg, you'd say, sure, he's the type, a guy who wants to be close to the action. He had trust-me eyes, a voice like honey in warm milk and a smile that melts ice cream. The kid was a winner, right? Wrong. The kid ended up in state prison.

Bojorquez, twenty-nine, lived gloriously for twenty-one champagne-filled days by charging it to Spielberg's Amblin Entertainment. He signed the tab for $800 dinners for himself and his friends at places like La Petit Château and La Serre. They dined on scampi, escargot, and wild duck. They drank Dom Perignon like there was no tomorrow. Nothing was too good for them. A 40 percent tip for the waiter. A limo to and from. Waiters and chauffeurs queued up to kiss his ring. Fame was a lady with a golden smile and a million-dollar ass, so let the good times roll.

When they stopped rolling, Bojorquez had charged more than five thousand dollars to Amblin Entertainment. There was only one catch. It was all a con, and it cost him eight counts of felony grand theft.

I caught up with Bojorquez in County Jail, just before they sent him up to do hard time. I asked why he did it and he shrugged. "It was stupid," he replied, eyes downcast, a small Bible tucked in the upper left-hand pocket of his prison greens. "It was a free ticket to fame. It got started, and I got caught up in it." He faced me suddenly. "I'm not comfortable with this. When I get out, things are going to be different."

He said it like he meant it, but then he said he worked for Spielberg like he meant it. Even his lawyer wasn't sure.

Bojorquez was waiting tables in the Valley when a friend employed by a movie company somehow discovered where Spielberg had charge accounts. He passed it on to Bojorquez, who decided to put the intelligence to good use. Oozing charm and self-confidence, both of which are necessary attributes of an accomplished con artist, he partied with impunity. None of the restaurants or limo companies asked questions when he told them he worked for Spielberg. You don't question 40 percent tips.

"It would flash on me at dinner, 'This isn't real,' " Bojorquez said, "but I didn't want to think about it, so I just had another drink."

When I asked what he'd say to Spielberg if he could, Bojorquez lowered his eyes again in studied atonement. "I'd tell him how sorry I was," he said. "I'd tell him I'm not proud of myself." Then he looked up, suddenly smiling the gleaming kid smile. "And I'd tell him I really like *E.T.* It was wonderful!"

FAME, DESPITE THOSE kinds of lapses, is taken very seriously in L.A., where it is a commodity to be set on a mantel or cashed at a bank. I visited a restaurant recently owned by Matty Danza, the brother of actor Tony Danza, whom I described in a column as an actor who appears in the kind of shows you watch when you've just had a cardiac bypass and are forced to lie on a couch for two weeks. A modestly amusing line, but not a fire starter. Well, first I got a telephone call from Matty, who accused me of using him to get to his brother. He showered me with invective and then hung up. The next call, left on my answering machine, was from a Sicilian who threatened to hand me back my nose, as he put it, and possibly other parts of my body, for having criticized Tony Danza.

In order to do that, I reasoned, he would have to remove those parts of my body he intended to hand back, *back* being the operative word. So I talked to a cop friend of mine and he said no one had the right to remove any part of my body I did not want removed. Then he laughed. He was not laughing at my fears, he explained, since they could be quite real and he would mention them to the LAPD stalking unit; he was only laughing at what I had written, the part about Tony Danza being in the kind of shows you watched . . . well, see above. Later, both Danzas said they had nothing to do with the threat to hand me back my body parts. It was simply a question of overenthusiasm on the part of Tony's fans. Since then, he's proved himself on the big screen as being better than the vehicles they gave him on television. In fact, he's pretty good. Maybe that'll save my nose.

I was also threatened for having made fun of actress Ali MacGraw, arguably the worst actress in America, who at the time was honorary mayor of Malibu, which gives you some idea how the City of the Stars regards leadership. Fans of Ali's considered it insulting when I referred to her as a member of Malibu's intelligentsia, properly concluding that I meant it in a sarcastic manner, which at least demonstrated a degree of understanding on their part. A woman caller who had loved Ali in *Love Story* screamed at me for several minutes, never drawing a breath or resorting to punctuations, and ended up by wishing that I would die bleeding from the mouth.

I didn't mention it to my cop friend, but I did mention it to Shortcut Bernstein, who said it was more of an expression of desire than an out-and-out threat and I should probably forget about it. I practically already have.

THERE IS MORE than one way to meet celebrities in L.A. Try, for instance, working in a business establishment frequented by the stars. Recently, for instance, I was pleased to have my 1992 Pontiac cleaned at a West Hollywood car wash patronized by people like Jay Leno and Morgan Fairchild. The proprietor, who is a man named, honest to God, Sunny Sunshine, is proud of his celebrity clientele and has their autographed pictures hanging on the wall just opposite the tunnel in which cars are automatically washed, rinsed, and hot-waxed. An exception is one photograph he keeps in his drawer. It is that of a former *Playboy* centerfold who is stark naked with nicely parted pubic hair, looking at the camera in a frontal view that is breathtaking.

Sunny Sunshine, who has had one heart attack and two cardiac bypass operations, says it is probably not a great idea for him to look at the picture too often since it causes a good deal of stress. His real first name, by the way, is Kalman, but he never uses it. I once knew a guard at the old MGM studios whose real name was Ken Hollywood, so Sunny Sunshine really doesn't throw me too much.

At any rate, by hanging around the Santa Palm Car Wash (named for its cross streets), you can see Leno, Arsenio Hall, Dom DeLuise, Johnny Mathis, Gene Hackman, and any number of others who are famous to one degree or another. Sometimes Sunny Sunshine has so many Rolls Royces going through his wash tunnel at one time that he wonders if he has enough insurance to cover them all should there be a disaster of some sort that impacts specifically on his business and their cars. Sunny likes them all, by the way, although he does mention that a few want their car washed as many as five times for the price of one and follow the finishing man around with a rag of their own to be sure that every spot is removed.

I don't wash cars or offer any other special service but do manage to meet celebrities right there in the city room of the *L.A. by God Times*. They come through to soak up atmosphere for projects they are about to embark on. Randy Quaid was the most recent. He spent a day with me preparing for the role of a columnist in *The Paper*.

Randy, not to be confused with his pretty brother Dennis, is a big, unassuming guy with a lopsided smile and the manner of a country preacher. You expected him to say "shucks" and dig his toe in the dirt. I don't think he's ever appeared in the *National Enquirer*, and to the best of my knowledge no one ever linked him to Heidi Fleiss or with any of the crowd who hangs out at the Viper Club or the Monkey Bar. People sometimes recognize him, that's for sure, but it is not for his beauty or for his stinging wit. Which is why I was surprised when they cast him to play the role of the columnist on *The Paper*. He's too, well, real, and who wants to see real in a movie? Most of us who write columns tend to be short and morose, but we would rather not be cast that way on film.

Quaid spent a day with me preparing for his role. I write columns mostly about people, rather than issues, so it doesn't require a lot of action. I don't carry a gun, track down criminals, or save anyone from being murdered. Even driving to where I'm going is lackluster. The most I might do would be to run over a dog in my company car, and I am careful not to do that. The paperwork would be murderous.

The best I could do in terms of action and contemporary violence was to take Quaid to the trial of Lyle and Erik Menendez, the brothers charged with murdering their parents one summer evening in 1989. They admitted killing them but claimed they did it to stop years of sexual and mental abuse. The prosecution said they did it to get their hands on a $14 million estate. Perish the thought.

The trial, which predated O.J., was the hottest ticket in L.A. at the time, and spectators lined up as early at two o'clock in the morning to get the limited number of seats available. It was seemingly an impossible dream to get into the courtroom in the afternoon, but I took Quaid there anyhow. A celebrity's face opens doors a lot faster than a press card. After halting me in a no-nonsense manner, the woman deputy sheriff guarding the door took one look at Quaid and decided there might be two seats available after all, if only for a limited time. As it turned out, however, the judge was hearing legal arguments and it was a waste of time as far as high drama was concerned. Legal arguments are not known for either action or humor.

The Menendez Brothers, like the Long Island Lolita, Amy Fisher, became celebrities by the simple expedience of committing a crime, in this case shooting their mama and their daddy. Book and movie deals were made all over town long before the case even went to the jury, which, according to Shortcut Bernstein, caused a lot of wannabes to consider shooting down a close relative of their own in order to achieve the kind of fame the brothers had come into. "One little squeeze of the trigger," Shortcut said, "and you're a Movie of the Week. Two squeezes and you're a mini-series."

I ALSO TOOK Quaid to visit a witch. She was a plumpish, middle-aged woman who called herself Devi and was the public relations priestess in the Coven of the Goddess, Inc. The idea that a group of witches could incorporate under the laws of the state didn't seem at all peculiar to me, having lived in California all my life. But a press agent for witches struck me as the ultimate historical attempt at revisionism. We've come a long way in the three hundred years since Salem, when they didn't have publicists to alter their image.

The reason I had lined up Devi was because a Disney movie called *Hocus Pocus* was in general release. It was the story of three witches who sought eternal youth by sucking the life essence from children. Devi wasn't like that. She became a witch in the '60s when strange things were popular, and unlike those who abandoned their interest in passing crusades like racial equality and world peace, she remained a witch. Today, with a degree in theater arts, she works in equity waiver houses and entertains at parties singing and doing standup comedy. A real L.A. witch.

Quaid listened to Devi with incredulous interest, as though he couldn't quite believe what he was hearing, the lopsided smile solidified on his face. Devi went on about how there were five thousand witches in L.A. and, contrary to the image projected in *Hocus Pocus,* they were good people who didn't engage in death, curses, or the drinking of human blood at their functions. A little Cabernet and some hors d'oeuvres was about as far as they'd go. What they actually did, other than sing and dance, was never made clear, but then, did it really matter?

I TOOK QUAID next to spend an hour with a woman named Tammy. She was the downside of L.A. In writing about this town you deal with a range of emotions that can leave anyone a little crazy. We mix fame with despair like no other city in the world, because they sleep together in a basin that encourages cohabitation. Mixing Quaid with Tammy was a perfect metaphor for L.A.: Quaid, famous and successful, and Tammy, dancing on the brink of the abyss.

A doper and a whore, hardly a day went by that Tammy, at thirty-four, didn't think of killing herself. She had tried it several times and dreamed about floating down a tunnel toward a white light of serenity she'd never known. She had used drugs since she was ten and had been on her own since she was twelve, selling her body to support a heroin habit that had reached three hundred dollars a day. She'd been beaten, raped, and robbed, and had spent more years in prison than she could remember.

She faced life like a wounded bird, and if there was a redeeming quality to her existence, it lay in her art. She drew strangely delicate and beautiful faces of women, their expressions a compelling blend of wonder and grief. And when she wasn't drawing them, a figure that emerged was the head of a unicorn, with a single tear on its face. It's a fantasy projection of her own distorted life, where even creatures of mythology cry.

The crooked smile, the gentle, down-home smile, faded from Quaid's face as he listened to the frail, edgy woman talk about how she sometimes closed her eyes and screamed, "God, get me out of this!" Quaid said very little when I drove him back to his car. I wondered what, if anything, he had absorbed from our encounters. The character he played in *The Paper* had nothing to do with what I showed him in L.A., but I guess a story like Tammy's would have never worked in a movie. Too real.

THERE ARE ALL kinds of people in L.A. who used-to-be. It isn't their fault. Fame, as Mark Twain knew, is a night vapor gone with sunrise. Only people like Steve Allen manage to keep it forever. He works at it by producing books at a prodigious rate and by writing songs and emceeing and being everywhere at once. I've never met anyone like Allen. His is a fame that never seems to fade, unlike television series leads whose faces appear on the faint edges of memory as someone we once knew but are unable to recall. You see them around town all the time, trying to muscle their way into a two-star restaurant by virtue of who they used-to-be, and failing. Tall men with hair pieces and women with face-lifts and butt-tucks, sad victims of fad's caprice.

Future used-to-bes abound in the City of Angles; those who enjoy a notoriety that lacks the substance to endure beyond next weekend. Old-timers in L.A. know that and don't take too seriously the media's breathless pursuit of someone like Heidi Fleiss, because they fade from the news like cow piss on a hot rock.

Even as I write, the Good Time Girl has dipped into temporary obscurity. Already sentenced to three years in prison for pandering, she awaits sentencing by a federal court for tax evasion and money laundering, convictions that could tack five years on to her pandering sentence unless pending appeals wipe them out. When she heard the federal verdict, she lowered her head and cried. The good life she came to symbolize was ending with a hangover.

Before her slip into obscurity, Heidi's court appearances involved media stampedes not witnessed before in L.A. (although O.J. has since outdone her), proving once more that sex still sells. Yet there is a sadness to the presence of the tiny Jewish girl whose own big mouth, police say, landed her in trouble. She was less than discreet about her "escort service" of beautiful young women, and indiscretion, while it lures fame, also brings notice. A sting operation by an undercover Beverly Hills detective finally brought her service to an end. Heidi Fleiss embarrassed the cops by flaunting her wares. They couldn't let her go.

Elizabeth (Alex) Adams could have taught Heidi a thing or two. She was the Beverly Hills Madam who managed to stay out of jail two years ago by becoming a police informant. Adams was not noisy. She ran a quiet operation out of her home high above Sunset Boulevard that, like Heidi's escort service, also catered to Middle East sheikhs and wealthy executives, though she is said to have avoided the show biz crowd. Heidi first attracted police attention when Adams accused her of stealing her wealthy clientele. The rest is water under the bed.

No scandal is ever wasted in L.A. Heidi took advantage of her notoriety by marketing a line of lingerie and sleepwear that bears her name. Featured is a pair of men's shorts with a pocket for condoms. AIDS activists don't know whether to condemn her immorality or praise her foresight. It doesn't matter. In the end, we all know where the skinny brunette will end up, even if she manages to stay out of jail. When the book is done and the television movie made and the underwear all sold, she'll be just another blip on the Hollywood radar screen, and blips are gone in a hurry.

TEN

There are only two modes of transport in Los
Angeles: car and ambulance.
—Humorist Fran Lebowitz

I KNEW DOWNTOWN was changing when the chicken boy disappeared. It was a twenty-three-foot-high plaster figure of a boy in overalls with a rooster head. It stood atop a chicken restaurant on Broadway, and though it wasn't the tallest edifice in town, it seemed somehow the most important. It was so . . . well . . . *L.A.*

When the restaurant failed some years ago, the chicken boy was carted off and stored, but its memory lingers on. Someone has produced a thirty-minute film, *Chicken Boy, the Movie,* and "The Chicken Boy Polka" has been recorded by an accordion band. We breathlessly await the Chicken Boy Rap.

The chicken boy is one of many landmarks lost to L.A. There was the Brown Derby restaurant on Wilshire in the shape of a derby, and a hot dog restaurant in the shape of a wiener and a doughnut restaurant that you entered through a hole, and so on. Programmatic architecture, it was called, created in the 1920s, '30s, and '40s, when we were all a little looser and a lot happier. Even murder seemed somehow more cheerful back then.

It was the chicken boy that characterized a downtown that, like the rest of L.A. at the time, was flat and a moldy gray, like refried beans left too long in the sun. I used to walk down Broadway when I first settled in L.A. It felt a lot like Tijuana. Mexican music floated out of almost every store and merged into one long *serenata* for three or so blocks from Times Mirror Square. The Million Dollar Theater, once a place of movie premieres, with spotlights and film stars, was given over to Spanish-language films. Crowded Grand Central Market, with its Latino-oriented foods, was the biggest game in town.

Off Broadway, Pershing Square still flourished. It was where old Bolsheviks stood atop park benches and told us why collectivism was the wave of the future, and where men of God in mismatched suits and home-done haircuts told us to prepare, for the end was near. Sometimes singers gathered in a corner of the square and sang for coins dropped in their guitar cases, while bums wandered about looking for handouts, in the days before we dignified them as homeless.

Then one day the chicken boy was gone. I noticed his absence on a day of discovery that began on Skid Row. I was writing about the Skid Row Slasher and wanted to describe what the down-and-out saw from the Row, a kind of view from the bottom. I looked westward and noticed for the first time how many tall buildings were spiking up out of the downtown skyline in the area around the old Biltmore, noticeably the sixty-two-story First Interstate Tower, the fifty-five-story Security Pacific Plaza and the gleaming black twin Arco Towers, fifty-two stories, that looked down on the poor like the devil's throne.

It was an epiphany I incorporated into the Slasher story, how those with nothing to lose but their lives existed in squalor in the shadows of symbols of wealth beyond their imagination. They could look up, if they looked up at all, to towers of opulence so removed from their daily lives that they were not unlike castles on a hill toward which peasants once gazed; where royalty waltzed and dined while they struggled and starved.

Up until 1956, no building was allowed to exceed thirteen stories in Los Angeles, except City Hall, which was twenty-eight stories. The city fathers figured that if an earthquake ripped through the downtown, people in the top floors of thirteen-story buildings wouldn't have as far to fall if their buildings toppled, compared to those in taller skyscrapers, proving once more that we don't elect civic leaders for either their intelligence or their ability to reason. New building materials and techniques, plus, no doubt, a little something from the builders into campaign funds, changed their minds, and high-rises entered into the lexicons of their conversations.

It all began in the 1970s, but it was sometime after that that I noticed the change. I'm not sure why I didn't realize it before, except that no one up until then paid a lot of attention to downtown L.A., except *San Francisco Chronicle* columnist Herb Caen, who came here looking for the city's center once and determined that it didn't exist. I went looking for it too after the Skid Row Slasher piece, and that's when I discovered the chicken boy was gone. You see how the two kind of went together? A realization that there were skyscrapers in L.A. and that yesterday had passed without my noticing.

We have a tendency to do that down here, to rip out the old and replace it with something that gleams. We're embarrassed by our own history, and hope that Something Better lies beyond the horizon of our future. I miss the chicken boy, though I'll admit a fascination with the new symbols of downtown L.A., beginning with the tallest building west of Chicago, the seventy-three-story First Interstate World Center, and a dozen other buildings that top forty floors. Now there's talk that someone wants to build the world's tallest tower, something like 122 stories, and I don't doubt they will. But it'll sure be one hell of a fall in an earthquake.

DOWNTOWN LOS ANGELES is bordered on three sides by an intricate tangle of freeways, and on the fourth by the concrete-banked L.A. River, an awkward slash of a waterway that never seems to fit into anyone's beautification plans, although a local legislator once wanted to turn it into a bicycle path. That idea went the way of one that proposed a hole in the San Gabriel Mountains to siphon smog out of the L.A. Basin and into Arizona. Smog was the result of a downtown designed for cars, not people, in the days when we abandoned existing mass transportation, the old Red Trains, for the independence of our own wheels.

The Pasadena Freeway was the first, a six-mile stretch from the suburbs into the central city, which, in the winter of 1940, seemed the ultimate answer to any transportation problem anyone would ever have. It was a new downtown then, too, when the chicken boy was young, before we had almost six million licensed drivers in the county choking our roads the way fat clogs a human artery. The Pasadena Freeway was called a miracle of ingenuity back then, and public transportation an infringement on our independence. We were in love with the car, and it has turned on us.

No one is certain why the downtown began dying, although the lack of adequate public transportation is certainly one reason. The east side of Broadway began to slowly rot, creating Skid Row out of the elegant old hotels and buildings that were the pride of L.A. when Hollywood was in its heyday. The suburbs began to build, first in the San Fernando Valley and then elsewhere, enticing those who wanted nothing to do with the sin and disrepair of urban life.

Downtown died in inverse proportion to the flourishing of the 'burbs with their easy parking and expansive malls, creating a breed of Angelino who had never even *seen* the downtown area. Downtown had become an island of contrasts, on one hand given over to government and commercial offices, on the other to junk shops and cheap clothing stores. Its population was largely Mexican, and still is, except for the Anglo edifices that have sprung up, like the lavish Music Center and the new Financial District that arose along with the skyscrapers of the '70s.

We create our own Skid Rows by turning our backs on segments of the population who no longer attract our interest. Because they dwell in economic brackets that allow their homes and apartments to fall into disrepair, we either label their dwellings slums and allow them to rot, or rip them out in the name of urban renewal. What we don't see won't hurt us, though we've learned the hard way that what we don't see now we'll see later in the crimes and riots that are handmaidens of despair.

That isn't to say treasures haven't existed in the downtown area. We had, and still have, Olvera Street, which is the birthplace of L.A., with its colorful shops and restaurants. We still have the ornate Union Station, once the hub of western rail traffic and now the refurbished center of a new train system. We still have the grandly baroque old Bradbury Building, the scene of a hundred movies and television episodes, Grand Central Market, the Garment District, the Flower Mart, the Produce Mart, Chinatown, and Little Tokyo.

They too withered during L.A.'s period of benign neglect and only recently have efforts been made to restore their earlier grandeur. The heart of one of the most important cities in the world, the queen of the Pacific Rim, is once more an interesting place to be. But you have to be able to get there first.

I DON'T KNOW how many times in the past thirty years the voters of Los Angeles have rejected bond issues aimed at building a transportation system beyond buses, the awkward, smelly vehicles that crawl like giant bugs around our freeways and surface streets. Every major city in the world, including Oakland, has a better system of public transportation than we have. Only now have we begun to build a web of subways and surface rail lines that can tie the county together from the farthest reaches of the San Fernando and San Gabriel Valleys to the ocean, and south to Long Beach.

Shortcut Bernstein has a theory that one of the reasons we don't have adequate rail transportation is that no one quite knows in which direction he's traveling in L.A. For instance, the Pacific Ocean, which is due west to most of California, is due south in Los Angeles, because of our geographic configuration . . . as of now, anyhow. There is that possibility, I suppose, that we will become an island if the earthquakes continue and we are set adrift as a separate landmass. Then the ocean would be all around us.

Meanwhile, however, the ocean is to the south. Therefore our main freeway, the Santa Monica, runs north and south. Except that the signs say east and west. The reason they say east and west is that the Ventura Freeway, which runs at right angles to the Santa Monica, also runs north and south. Well, it does most of the time. There are also signs that say it runs east and west.

Let me put it this way. Picture in your mind a cross. The horizontal portion of the cross is the Santa Monica. The vertical part is the Ventura. Now simply assume that they both run north and south and east and west depending upon where you are at any given time. If you are at the intersection of the cross, your location is impossible to describe. You could be anywhere. I haven't even mentioned the San Diego Freeway, which also runs north and south and intersects the Santa Monica at a point where it also runs north and south, and the Golden State, which also runs north and south.

Well, you get the idea. It isn't so important exactly where you are in L.A. or where you're going, as long as you're going to the right places. By the way, the right places are all on the city's west side, which is also the south side if you're getting there by freeway. Go figure.

Shortcut's theory of relative direction notwithstanding, we are at last getting rail transportation in the City of Last Resort. It's a modest beginning, to be sure, but about five hundred years from now all corners of the county, and then some, ought to be tied together from north to south and north to south with 150 miles of integrated surface-subway tracks that will take our inheritors anywhere they want to go, even the San Fernando Valley if it's still there.

It began on a blistering summer Sunday in 1990 with the opening of a twenty-two-mile light rail track running from L.A. to Long Beach, a city to the south once famous for its intoxicated sailors, Howard Hughes's wooden seaplane, the *Spruce Goose,* and the *Queen Mary.* It is not so much a fleet town anymore, the *Spruce Goose* is up in the northwest someplace now, and there's talk that the *Queen Mary* may be relocated, too. Possibly by the time of publication, Long Beach will be renowned for nothing more than being the southern terminal of L.A.'s rail line. Let it go at that. It already pisses off San Diego, Santa Barbara, and Bakersfield to be thought of as suburbs of L.A., and this will just add one more group of people who wish to hell we'd sink into the sea.

The Long Beach connection is called the Blue Line. The simplicity of the name astounded me. I thought it might be the Lucille Ball or the Humphrey Bogart Line, so given are we in L.A. to applying the names of movie stars, past and present, to streets, structures, and services. A critic who thinks it's all a terrible waste of money calls it "a streetcar named disaster." But the Blue Line was good enough for 25,000 people to turn out on opening day to see what the Rapid Transit District had wrought for almost a billion dollars along the same route once used by the Red Car trolleys, junked thirty years ago as obsolete in favor of the shiny new freeways, three of which were turned to rubble by a 6.8 earthquake.

Two and a half years after the Blue Line came the Red Line. It's a 4.4-mile subway that has cost $1.4 billion and taken twenty years to build, from inception to operation. Well, it's a start. The Red Line also opened on a sunny Sunday. A crowd twice the size of the Blue Line mob gathered to hear then-Mayor Tom Bradley announce: "The Red Line will take us into the twenty-first century." Someday, no one is betting when, there will be 22.7 miles of subway under L.A. None of the stations, however, will have bathrooms. Crime festers in bathrooms. You're just going to have to hold it until you get to Burbank.

This is not our first subway, by the way. A one-mile Hollywood subway opened in 1925 and closed thirty years later, still only one mile long. But no one was thinking about that old thing when the crowds gathered and when taped music played "Stars and Stripes Forever." I personally have never ridden on the Red Line because its 4.4 miles don't go anywhere I want to be. I did ride the Blue Line once, but vowed never to do so again when security officers arrested a man for eating a cough drop at one of the stations, where there's a no-eating rule. The man insisted he was sucking the cough drop, not eating it, but no one cared. It was in his mouth, and that's eating. He could have been fined $750, but the judge dismissed the case with a warning to anyone who might come before her again with the cough drop defense. Next time, she will not be so merciful.

To those who wish Hollywood would go to hell, it seemed headed that way when subway tunneling under its main thoroughfare, Hollywood Boulevard, allowed the ground to sink ten inches, causing cracked walls, sunken floors, and broken pipes. It shut down the subway project for several months and has caused a barrelful of lawsuits. The Metropolitan Transportation Authority, which is responsible for L.A.'s transit system, wasn't having a sweet time of it to begin with.

Merchants were already complaining that business was off due to the construction, and sinking streets weren't helping.

To ease their pain, the MTA hired carolers at Christmas and trucked in four tons of snow, but that didn't stop the bitching or the flow of claims against the project. Naked elves doing flips in the gutters wouldn't have stopped that. Hollywood Boulevard is used to naked elves doing flips in the gutters. It's no big deal.

Only one voice seemed to be raised in defense of the chaos that accompanied the subway problems. An architect demanded of a businessman along the boulevard, "Do you want to be in the heart of the metropolis, where the world economy is right outside your door? Or do you want to be in Cucamonga listening to the birds chirp?" While there is no record of his reply, the birds are sounding better all the time.

TO ADD TO the rainbow of colors that form our transportation web, we will also ultimately have something called the Green Line, which will be another surface rail system on twenty miles of track that will take whoever wants to go to from El Segundo to Norwalk, two nondescript communities in the southern, or western, part of the county. The line will cost in the neighborhood of $800 million to take 25,000 passengers a day from nowhere to nowhere, but, what the hell, it's only money. L.A.'s subway project, the most expensive per mile in U.S. history, will end up costing at least $5 billion and will continue pissing people off until after the year 2000, so what's another million? Pocket change.

Then there's something called Metrolink now, which are trains that run on two hundred miles of Amtrak rails from locations in four counties to downtown's Union Station near Olvera Street, where L.A. was born. Metrolink carries about ten thousand riders a day, a figure that increased when the earthquake of '94 wiped out the Golden State Freeway.

Since the Metrolink service began in 1992 there have been ten train-related deaths. Four of them were suicides, leading Shortcut Bernstein to speculate that we may have something in Metrolink to match the notoriety of San Francisco's Golden Gate Bridge, where almost a thousand humans have swan-dived to their deaths. Well, there were a few jackknives too and some belly flops, I assume, among the less athletically inclined. The point is, leaping in front of an oncoming train may prove as popular as jumping off the Golden Gate, thus saving many the airfare of flying to San Francisco to end it all. The L.A. Chamber of Commerce might well include a bumper sticker in its packet to "Do It in L.A."

The idea is eventually to tie the Green, Blue, and Red Lines in with Metrolink so that those coming into downtown L.A. will be able to get where they want to go. But, I hear you ask, once they reach downtown, where on earth will they go? Good question.

I FIRST VISITED L.A. in 1947 in the summer between high school graduation and the start of college. I was in the Marine Corps Reserves doing two weeks in San Diego, and two of us hitchhiked to L.A. for the weekend. We were looking for Hollywood (wasn't everyone back then?), but somehow ended up in Pershing Square. It was, and still is, a square block park pretty much in the middle of the city across from the Biltmore Hotel and on the edge of the Jewelry Mart. There were bums there and winos and all the rest of the human flotsam I mentioned earlier.

But it was a colorful place, too, with noise and music and grand debates on socialism, religion, and whether or not free love was a viable way to prevent rape and prostitution. My buddy and I received a lot of attention because we were in our uniforms, which, just two years after World War II, still held the respect of the crowd. Twice we were offered drinks from half-pint bottles of whiskey tucked in coat pockets, and we took them both times. The second time was from a guy named Harry who told us stories about his war, back in 1918, and how he'd taken shrapnel in the groin and had emerged from the war only half the man he'd been when he went in.

We slept in Pershing Square that night near a statue of Ludwig van Beethoven, because those were the days you could do that kind of thing without risking a bullet in your head from some clown flying on speed or acid or something worse. The night was as balmy as a tropical island and a quarter moon sailed over the old Biltmore as we drifted off listening to music playing somewhere. . . .

I mention all that because Pershing Square changed sometime after that. The harmless old bums and winos were chased off by a more dangerous kind of homeless people who were freed from institutions when California decided it wasn't going to warehouse loonies anymore. The dope dealers came, too, and the square became a kind of flea market for drugs, the way MacArthur Park is on the western edge of town. Crime became a way of life day or night, until the city decided the Pershing Square that existed—where guys like Harry hung out, dreaming of their lost manhood—just didn't fit into plans for a new downtown.

So they tore it out and rebuilt it at a cost of $15 million. Now you've got a purple carillon tower rising over the square with a pink globe on its pinnacle. There's a yellow-walled open-air café, citrus trees, a rose-tinted walkway, and a waterfall. The only thing left of the old square is the Beethoven statue and some war memorials. Everything else is different. It's the new downtown. Even the Biltmore has been refurbished.

I'm not saying it's good and I'm not saying it's bad. God knows, the dealers and the crazies had to go, but a little more of the natural look might have been nice, without the blinding purples and the rosy walkways. Thank God they left the old central library, third-largest in the nation, in more or less its original state. The place burned down in 1986, which required a rebuilding plan that added a lot of new, like the striking glass-domed atrium, but kept much of the old, too. People who probably never read a book in their lives helped clean up the mess the fire made before the rebuilding started.

The new downtown seems to be reflecting the old-new attitude. Old theaters are being restored as new towers rise, and there's even a link that connects older parts of the city with the new high-rise district. It's the Mediterranean-style Bunker Hill Steps, an updated replica of Rome's old Spanish Steps, sweeping down a hillside like cascading water between tall buildings, with broad landings, streams, and even an open-air café on one side. At the top there's a hotel, an art museum, and a lot of other attractions the city is betting will lure tourists.

I'll grant you it may seem a bit glitzy to those unfamiliar with the way we think out here, but that's probably the way it should be. L.A. is L.A., and that very concept embraces glitz the way Yves Montand embraced Marilyn Monroe in *Let's Make Love*. We're still one damned big movie, and even if the Ultimate Earthquake does wipe out everyone in the city but one pair of lovers, you'll find them in the last sunset, holding hands until twilight comes, and greeting the night with a kiss.

ELEVEN

If you tilted the whole country sideways, Los Angeles is the place where everything loose would fall.
—Anonymous

THE FIRST IMMIGRANTS to what is now L.A. arrived in 1781, forty-four in all. They came from Sonora, Mexico, by order of the Spanish government, to help strengthen Spain's hold on what is now California in what is now the United States on what is now Planet Earth. They joined a small group of what is now known as Native Americans and founded the city of El Puebla de Nuestra Señora la Reina de los Angeles de Porciuncula—the town of our lady the queen of the angels of Porciuncula. But for a twist of fate, we might be Porciuncula today instead of Los Angeles.

A short while later, the immigrants took over control of the area and crowded the Native Americans into a ghetto, then took the ghetto away from them and built high-rises and condos and multi-level garages on what had been their homes and their sacred burial sites, trampling on their culture, their religion, and, if they got in the way, on them. Things haven't changed much.

In modern L.A., there is still trouble between the natives and the immigrants, except that now the natives are in charge. So the idea is to throw out the immigrants, or at least throw out the illegal immigrants, and charge everyone else a one-dollar "transit fee" to cross the border into the good old U.S. of A. This applies mostly to those from Latin America because, well, there are just so damned many of them. Give me your huddled masses yearning to breathe free, but, God willing, they will come mostly from white countries like England and Denmark.

I was an immigrant from Oakland at a time of raised consciousness to what is regarded in Anglo L.A. as Our Hispanic Heritage. As a result, I was welcomed with open arms until the raised consciousness came crashing to the ground under the weight of a new wave of anti-immigrationism. No one seems quite sure why this is happening, though the recession and the struggle for work, especially in Southern California, has a lot to do with it. There were the riots, too, after which a brief period of ethnic euphoria faded into new and growing hatreds between blacks and Latinos, and now blacks and Asians, too, as well as the more traditional hatreds between blacks and whites.

In addition, we have escalating animosities between all of the aforementioned groups and newly arrived immigrants from the Arab nations, who seem to own all of the gas stations and the convenience stores in town. Their daughters work as bank tellers, which, as you might imagine, turns the simple need to deposit money into a communications nightmare between two diverse cultures, but not without elements of humor.

Consider one situation at a Bank of America when I tried to put twenty-five dollars into my savings account. It did not seem at the outset a complicated matter. It was not laundered money or money created in someone's basement with counterfeit plates. But accents and idioms seized the moment and confusion ensued. The teller, who looked Kuwaiti, handed me a piece of paper at the end of our business and said what sounded like "Wazashee canalonie." I said, "I beg your pardon?" and she repeated the phrase, this time as a question, "Wazashee canalonie?" It was obvious from the tilt of her head and the look in her eyes that she expected an answer. Her fingers were poised over a computer keyboard.

I could have repeated "Wazashee canalonie" in a bold, declarative manner and let it go at that, hoping it would somehow work out. It is a technique I employ when faced with the unknown. But this was a bank, and banks are no place to fool around.

"Look," I said, taking it from the top, "I only want to deposit twenty-five dollars in my savings account. It's for a trip to Bermuda." She seemed confused, so I raised my voice. Foreigners understand better when you shout at them. "PUT THE TWENTY-FIVE DOL-LARS IN," I hollered, "AND GIVE ME BACK MY DEPOSIT BOOK AND I'LL LEAVE!"

An armed guard at the far end of the bank was beginning to take notice. Lord help me if he thought I'd said, "PUT ALL THE MONEY IN A PAPER BAG AND NO ONE WILL GET HURT!" *Hollering Bandit Hits Town. Film at 11.*

I gave up. I sighed and said, "Wazashee canalonie," signed the piece of paper without reading it, accepted my bank book, and left. The teller said, "Thank you please." I said, "Welcome to America."

TWO YEARS HAVE passed since the 6.8 earthquake shook us into a more religious mode in the City of Angles, praise the Lord. It is said in combat that there are no atheists in foxholes, and that holds true during a disaster, either natural or man-made. There was more talk of God during and after the quake than I've ever heard before, though many have also lifted their arms and their voices to extraterrestrials, which they are certain will come to save them during a disaster on Planet Earth, sing hallelujah! Space creatures represent a different kind of alien, and just how their migration might be handled has yet to be seen, though I suspect that welcoming ceremonies will be quickly followed by an Earth for Earthlings campaign.

After the earthquake, as after the riots, love bloomed amid the ruble. We helped one another regardless of race, color, or political persuasion. Ethnic lines vanished because everyone was in the same leaky boat together. There was a lot of trans-ethnic hugging and understanding and sharing of limited essentials because the epicenter of the shaker was in a culturally mixed section of Anglos, Arabs, Latinos and African Americans. If you shared with or hugged anyone at all, statistically it was likely to be someone unlike yourself, which, in hindsight, must cause bigots a good deal of distress.

The euphoria began to fade with the diminishing aftershocks and the long lines for grants, loans, and food stamps. Pretty soon we were asking, hey, just how many of these people in line are *real* Americans and not illegal immigrants? The question evolved into a suggestion in the nation's capital, echoed by Our Wimp in Sacramento, to deny long-term earthquake assistance to those who are in this country illegally. Forget that their homes have been shaken into debris and that their jobs no longer exist and that their babies have no food; give 'em a gallon of distilled water, a food packet, and send them on their way. They're damned lucky to have short-term relief. No need to give 'em grants to exist beyond the fading memory of the quake itself. In the following election, the whole state formalized Anglo hostility toward everyone brown by voting in Proposition 187, denying education and health benefits to illegal immigrants, and hinting that they'd like to get the legal ones, too. So much for transethnic love.

That situation symbolizes what's going on now in L.A. when it comes to our attitude toward immigrants. They'll tell you that by immigrants they mean *illegal* immigrants, and that's different than legal immigrants, who get less brown as time passes. Legal, schmegal, the anti-immigrationists mean people with dark skin who don't speak the language. As proof, a member of the L.A. County Board of Supervisors, who is black, initiated an ordinance making it illegal for people to gather on street corners or in public parking lots in search of jobs. Rejected at first, it subsequently passed, creating yet another method of polarizing our population.

Though ethnic background isn't mentioned, the people who gather and offer themselves up as workers are 99 percent Latinos, most from Mexico. They'll work their tails off for five dollars an hour doing whatever it is you want them to do, from digging holes to building houses. Many are gifted craftsmen who study English at night and send money home to support their families. But, well, they're brown-skinned, and they have this funny accent, so let's get the cholos the hell out of there.

The new county law, by the way, does not address the bums, mostly Anglo, who beg on just about every street corner and free-

way offramp in L.A. and who, by their unyielding demand for
money, have become a menace to just about everyone. Offer them
jobs and they'll decline because they're veterans and thereby emo-
tionally unfit to take actual physical work. We call them homeless
and tolerate them because they're white, and go after those damned
Mexicans instead.

The anti-immigration attitude, ignited by recession and fueled by
riots and maybe, in the post-euphoria period, by the earthquake, too,
has been enhanced by both President Clinton and California's whis-
pery Governor Pete Wilson, by both of the state's U.S. Senators,
and by others scattered throughout Southern California. It was one
of our Senators, Dianne Feinstein, who suggested we charge everyone one dollar to cross our borders, a notion that would have been
hooted into oblivion during normal times, but which gathered ad-
herents due to the racist temper of the times. Someone suggested
that the crossing from Mexico be limited to one entryway. The an-
ticipated miles-long line would be controlled by utilizing the kind
of zigzag arrangement employed at Disneyland and other happy-place
theme parks. Balloons and hats are optional.

About two years ago, a reporter for CNN writing about im-
migration called and wanted to know whether I thought anti-
immigrationism would turn into a real problem in L.A. I said no,
that I thought we were made of better stuff; we were, after all, a
classically multicultural society, and we were proud of it. Ask anyone. Now that I look around and read my mail and talk to the people I thought were card-carrying liberals, I've got to say I was at least
partially wrong. There's a problem all right. Hatred has become popular.

I AM LED to believe there is a cookbook in L.A. on how to prepare
dogs. It was mentioned to me by Shortcut Bernstein, who never did
come up with the actual book but claimed to be able to quote some
of the recipes. It was supposedly printed for the benefit of immigrant
Asians who love dog meat. I can't imagine eating my own dog
Hoover, who is as ugly as a manatee . . . but then, come to think of

it, a cow isn't exactly a thing of beauty, and American culture is fueled by Big Macs.

Verification of dog-eating in L.A. came from animal activist Barbara Fabricant, the widow of Sid the Squid, a racetrack tout who died some years ago. When they buried him they sprinkled shredded racing forms over his coffin and played tapes of famous races at Hollywood Park. Barbara says that certain Asians bail dogs out of the pound then take them home and cook them. It's cheaper than ground round and, well, 100 percent of what it claims to be: dog meat.

Shortcut says he saw recipes for dog foo-yung and dog-kabob in the book, whose name or publisher he cannot recall, though he suggests laughingly the title could be, *How Much Is That Doggie in the Meat Case?* One recipe, he claims, stretched to another culture and came up with Cajun dog steak. Intriguing, but I doubt that it will ever replace blackened redfish as the next haute cuisine.

I sought a copy of the book by mentioning it in a column, but instead received a mountain of mail condemning me for making light of so heinous a practice as eating one's pet. One letter-writer suggested I "picture a family in Vietnam taking a trusting, very much alive dog on a picnic, playing with it until lunchtime, hanging it from a tree to die, and burning its fur from its body with a torch in preparation for the barbecue pit."

I found it personally difficult to visualize, but I suppose it would be the Western equivalent of taking your chicken on a picnic, feeding it grain, watching it peck about happily with the kids, then lopping off its head, plucking its feathers and eating it for lunch. Placed in that context, I can visualize it a little better, though I remain unmoved by the outrage. Different cultures have different practices.

We accept that premise in L.A. during good times, because we have become accustomed to our ethnic mix. The county of 9 million souls breaks down into 3.5 million Latinos, 1 million Asians, and 1 million African Americans. By last count, we have 250,000 Chinese, 143,000 Koreans, 61,000 Vietnamese, 223,000 Filipinos, and 130,000 Japanese. The rest of the people represent varying shades of white: fleecy-white, lily-white, off-white, milk-white, ivory-white, maggot-white, chalk-white, and as white as the driven snow.

I isolate the Asian population to point out that we also have an estimated 500,000 dogs in L.A. County. That comprises one-half dog for each Asian, although, of course, they don't all eat animals. Some are possibly even vegetarians. I don't know how many vegetarians there are in the county, though I suspect there are at least as many vegetarians as there are Asians, and twice as many as there are dogs.

SUNSET BOULEVARD IS a microcosm of the city mix from Chinatown westward: past the Mexicans and Central Americans in Echo Park, the Armenians and Soviet Jews in Hollywood, and the Europeans and Asians in upscale Brentwood and Pacific Palisades. Many brought their cultures with them and opened stores and restaurants featuring foods that appeal especially to them. I'm not just talking tacos or sushi here, but hog maws, cow heads, pig snouts, duck feet, and bogor nuts.

I'm talking pork bellies, blood sausage, bagoongs, mung beans, bocconcini, fustolt szalona, roggereye, smoked sprat, krupuk, apfel korn, basmati rice, sfogliatelle, yaki karei, dangmyun noodles, kimchi, cotijo cheese, fish balls, and snapping eels.

There are ethnic enclaves all over this big, sprawling city, from Little Tokyo to Koreatown, from East L.A. to Filipino Town, from Little India to the Alpine Village, from black South Central to the Jewish Fairfax District, and their restaurants all serve foods dear to the hearts of their immediate population. A few upscale eating places combine different ethnic foods, like Chinese and Italian, French and Japanese, and, God help us, Mexican and Thai. But what best characterizes the town is the kosher burrito, which kind of says it all. If we are what we eat, I don't know what the hell we are. There's a Japanese burrito, too, but it hasn't caught on yet.

THE MOST ETHNICALLY diverse area of L.A. is probably the San Fernando Valley, and I'm not just talking about the diversity of ethnic gangs. About ninety different languages are spoken by students in L.A.'s Unified School District, and almost all of them are represented in the Valley. English and Spanish dominate, along with other Indo-European languages, including Welsh, Albanian, Armenian, and Farsi. *Whaaat?* Farsi. It's Persian. Oh.

Twenty thousand kids speak Tagalog, the chief native language of the Philippines, 17,000 speak Korean, 10,000 speak Chinese, 8,500 speak Arabic, and 8,000 speak Sanskrit, Hindi, or Nepali. A little surfer is spoken in the West Valley, dude, though the predominance of sun-speak is limited mostly to the oceanfront, of which, alas, there is none in the Valley. The two least-spoken languages in Valley schools are American Indian and Mon-Khmer.

You've got to figure if the kids are speaking this in school, there's a mama and/or papa at home and possibly some aunts, uncles, and maybe grandparents who speak the same language and enjoy the same cultural traits. They shop at the aforementioned stores, eat at ethnic restaurants, read ethnic newspapers, and watch ethnic television. There are about fifty different newspapers available to our ethnic groups, from Armenian to American Indian, and television stations that cater to everyone from Samoans to Asians.

KMET-TV is L.A.'s newest television station specializing in multilingual programming. Since half of the people in L.A. County speak a language other than English at home, Channel 38 is a hit, offering programs in Italian, German, Russian, Spanish, Korean, French, Hindi, Japanese, Tagalog, African, and Spanish . . . and it's still reaching out. Using a telephone as a mike, you can sing along with "The Interactive Karaoke Show" or dance to African juju music, and no one's going to think you're odd. That's just the way we are.

But, despite the lyrical nature of L.A.'s language mix, we still keep trying our damnedest to homogenize it all into perfect English, or at least the native idiom that is as close to the Mother Tongue as mid-American can get. As a result, there's a fortune being made teaching English to the world's immigrants who end up in the City of Angles. And at least one company created by a speech pathologist offers "accent reduction" to those from abroad who want to blend in. I have a tendency to mumble, and when I called one day the secretary thought I was saying my name was Elmer Teenez. She men-

tioned that I might want to register for a course on language artic-
ulation.

Despite all the efforts to homogenize, I figure it will take another
hundred years for everyone to sound alike in L.A. and possibly a hundred thousand years for everyone to look alike and a million years
for everyone to be named Chang. The last prediction comes from
Shortcut Bernstein, who gets it from a defrocked Jesuit who says we
are running out of original names and tending to overuse those we
already have. So eventually everyone will be named the same. Shortcut wasn't sure how he came up with Chang, but does it matter?

IF THERE STILL remains doubt that L.A. is a global village, look around.
Ethnic diversity coupled with an ever-loosening lifestyle has resulted
in a kind of cultural fashion explosion, with everyone wearing who
he is. She too. I'm not talking the baggy-pants grunge look that
gangs and mentally deficient teenagers affect, but the kind of clothing that has become an ethnic statement.

In the two decades that I have been, you'll forgive the term, an
Angeleno, we've gone from Hawaiian shirts and checkered shorts
to turbans, Guatamalan shirts, saris, and hand-painted sandals from
Pakistan. This is true not only in weird places like Hollywood and
Malibu, but also in the straight world downtown and in the finan-
cial sections of the Greater Metropolitan San Fernando Valley.

Most businesses, bowing to the post-quake euphoria of loving eth-
nics, have abandoned the notion of suits and ties to allow a freer style
of clothing in the workplace. L.A. has always tended in that direction, being a cross between Miami Beach and Omaha, mostly based
on the fact that we have always been noticeably devoid of style, but
also because our temperature range is eternally in the low to middle eighties.

But now no one even looks up if you come to work in Peruvian
jackets adorned with red llamas or two-piece African butterfly
dresses and head wraps or Kufi hats or dangly East Indian jewelry or
Nehru jackets. We call it the unconstructed look, and it includes
everything from synthetic dreadlocks to Guatemalan surf wear.

Crafty entrepreneurs, cashing in on the trend, encourage it by stocking imports from throughout the world, thus turning ethnic statements into ethnic styles. Just as the whispering white boys from upper-class Bel-Air are wearing gang styles, whitebread adults from the same neighborhood are affecting African dashikis and American Indian turquoise.

It's a whole new world, and most of it is right here in old El Lay, amigo. And while there's friction, that will also fade, and so too will those who stir pots of ethnic hatred to the benefit of no one. Love and hope will bloom among the palm trees in the years to come, because how you gonna create hatred when everybody's name is Chang?

TWELVE

*I don't mind that I'm fat. I still get the
same money.*
—Marlon Brando

I WAS STANDING in front of a full-length mirror looking at myself in profile. I was just out of the shower and naked. I studied myself from double chin to potbelly, ignoring the rest. It was not a pretty sight. I have allowed myself to go to hell. Where is the slim, agile young person who once walked in my shoes? It is a question asked often of themselves by both men and women in a city that celebrates flat tummies and sharply edged jawlines. Courtney Cox and Brad Pitt are this year's look. I am twenty pounds overweight and it has settled in all the wrong places. In L.A. we equate obesity with leprosy. Fat people are not invited to Malibu parties. Fat people do not get the best tables at the Beverly Hills Bistro. Fat people drive Pontiacs.

If nothing else, L.A. is in shape. That's because it's a show biz town, and everyone wants to look like the slim beauties that grace our screens and our picture tubes. As a result, every new diet that comes down the Hollywood pike is tried here first with verve and enthusiasm . . . and mixed results. Take the three-day canned beet, cauliflower, tuna, and hot dog diet. For a while, everyone was locked into a regimen of eating things they didn't like because it promised instant weight loss. Beets and cauliflower top the list. It was the first time I had ever seen anyone actually chew and swallow a beet, and there were some in L.A. who had never heard of cauliflower.

It was called the Kaiser Permanente Diet and it was sweeping Southern California. You ate a hard-boiled egg for breakfast, a cup of cottage cheese and three crackers for lunch, and a mix of tuna, hot dogs, beets, and cauliflower for dinner on different nights. This went on for three out of every seven days, and you were supposed to end up looking like your own daydream. Your cholesterol level would plummet overnight to the standard of an Olympic distance runner. God would love you, and you'd marry Cindy Crawford or Keanu Reeves, or maybe both of them. Unfortunately, the whole thing could rot your insides and cause death.

I first heard of the diet from a comedy writer who worried, among other things, about what he perceived to be his obesity. The man was borderline anorexic. He weighed 140 pounds and was six feet tall and had not an ounce of fat on him. But comedy writers are haunted people and not to be trusted on matters of health. I telephoned Kaiser Hospital to learn if, indeed, they had created the diet. A spokesman was appalled. He said they had not and, in fact, such a diet could cause ketosis, which could lead to internal rotting, kidney failure, and the aforementioned death. But, then again, you could lose weight. It was a trade-off. I tried it and lost twenty pounds and didn't die. Then I said to hell with it and gained thirty pounds. I hate beets.

Within three months beets were out and we waddled on to something else.

EVERYONE HAS A favorite diet. The Pritikin Diet is probably the most severe. Tofu and lima beans soaked in rainwater are among its staples. Cardiologists recommend the Pritikin Diet along with a program of exercise that has felled strong men. Why die from heart failure when you can die of treadmill exertion? There is no fat in the Pritikin regimen. If a cow enters, you are to leave the room instantly. Dessert consists of "fun little rice crackers." Everything is tasteless.

As severe as it is, however, it still might be better than the Burbank Diet. Try mixing ice cream and fish in one unpalatable dish and you'll see what I mean. It's called the fish split. The collation is like a banana split in which the banana is replaced with a whole cooked fish lying between mounds of ice cream. The fish has a cherry in its mouth and whipped cream along its unscaled back.

The Burbank Diet comes from a book of the same name by one Lola Peters. Its basic strategy is based on the theory of "noxious combining." The idea is to make food so disgusting that the crudest of individuals will not want to eat it. There are some things that even catsup won't save. Other examples: strawberries and cream combined with prairie oysters and, under "gourmet noxious," chocolate mousse and headcheese. A "hearty-man Jell-O platter" features a combination so vile I will spare you a precise description, except to ask that you imagine yourself eating a live monkey smothered in peanut butter.

I wrote about the Burbank Diet and was amazed at the number of people willing to try it. Some readers offered their own disgusting combinations. Calf's liver and sliced peaches was one. Others offered diets that had worked for them, including those centered around wine, mashed potatoes, broccoli, water, seaweed (which also works in the Burbank Diet), tree moss, pond scum, cranberry juice, alfalfa sprouts, 100 proof gin, and human blood. The blood was suggested by a man who claimed he was a vampire and had not had a medical problem for four hundred years. He was from Hollywood.

WHEN DENNIS QUAID lost forty-three pounds in three months for his role as the tubercular Doc Holiday in *Wyatt Earp*, everyone wanted to know how he did it. The movie wasn't a smash, but the diet was. Unfortunately, however, it isn't as easy as the Burbank Diet or as accessible as the Pritikin Diet. Both a nutritionist and a physician guided Quaid through the process, which included limiting him to 1,200 calories a day, avoiding fat, drinking rivers of water, and undertaking a program of aerobic exercises that would leave a less-driven man in a state of physical collapse. But making a movie, like levitating or raising the dead, requires an emotional dedication beyond the abilities of ordinary people. There are actors in this town who would gladly swallow poison just to play the role of a dead man in a B-movie.

Exercise was the key to Quaid's success, as it is in most diets, even the Burbank Diet. Quaid walked nine miles a day and used a stair-climber, which is even more boring than a treadmill. In the Burbank Diet, Peters suggests a variety of ways by which one can burn calories. They include family fights (138 for jumping up and down, 249 for faking a heart attack) and a series the author calls "putting on the dog." In this, one literally drapes the family dog over one's shoulder and walks twenty paces. The amount of calories burned range from 12 for using a Pekingese to 227 for a Saint Bernard. I tried it with Hoover and he bit the back of my head, stupid dog.

The book also suggests sex as a means of weight control. Peters writes, "Sex is fun, sex is fulfilling, and best of all, sex is nonfattening. The Burbank Diet endorses sex and plenty of it, especially at mealtimes." There is no specific benefit mentioned by Peters, but I recall reading in *Life* magazine that a normal sex act burns 150 calories. That was a long time ago. Since then, brave new methods of sexual satisfaction have been discovered in Los Angeles, including the use of weights, vitamin injections, and trampolines, leading to the belief that the number of calories burned during the course of intercourse has doubled and possibly tripled. Some may argue this is not normal sex, but what may seem abnormal in Omaha is perfectly acceptable in L.A. The Butterfly Position and the Macrobiotic Carrot are moving eastward slowly, but they haven't reached Nebraska yet.

ANY DISCUSSION OF exercise must invariably include running. I doubt that any city in the world fields as many amateur runners as L.A. Everyone runs. Mothers run pushing strollers. Fathers run walking dogs. Senior-citizen organizations feature runfests. Singles clubs have runalongs. Valley Girls run in malls. We are not talking evening and weekends here. We are talking every minute of every day of the year, no matter what. I have seen runners trotting down the darkened streets at three in the morning with flashlights in their hands and reflectors on their asses. Jogging suits with luminous stripes and shoe heels with blinking lights are among other safety features that prevent them from being run down by drivers trying to find their way home after the bars close. One or two still become road-kill every year, but even though the accidents are fatal, they die knowing that favorable statistics are on their side. There are still more runners on the road than there are bodies.

The importance of running in L.A. was brought home during the '94 quake. The earth had barely stopped moving when the runners hit the streets. They were puffing down the avenues even as buildings were still collapsing and survivors were being dug out of the rubble. They carried hand weights and bottles of Evian water out on routine morning jogs that circumvented the nuisance of an earthquake, trotting over or around the rubble and the bodies as necessity required.

Their presence during the quake didn't surprise me. I was on Malibu Canyon Road during the previous year's wildfires that burned with devastating effect through the Santa Monica Mountains. Media credentials allowed me to get reasonably close to the disaster area, though even then I managed to maintain a safe distance. I don't want to die in a fire. I want to go like Emmett Turner, who was a political activist whose liver gave out on him a few years back. He decided as he neared the end that he wanted the life-support machinery that kept him alive to be unplugged. He wanted that and a Beefeater martini, very dry and straight up, with two olives. He died with the martini half-drunk and the olives uneaten.

I was right on the edge of the most disastrous fire in L.A. history, too close for my own comfort, when out of the smoke and heat, like a creature from hell, came a runner. He was wearing shorts and a T-shirt and those hundred-dollar air-cushioned running shoes that Malibu people favor, and carried the traditional bottle of Evian water. His appearance through great quantities of smoke made him seem, in addition to a runner from hell, a creation of special-effects experts who were able to somehow superimpose him in the smoke after taping him in a safe and smoke-free environment. Even the firefighters were startled to see the guy emerge from the chaos of fire and watched him trot down the canyon with their mouths half-open.

Later, I saw other runners along the Pacific Coast Highway, which was crammed with fire-fighting equipment. They had to be careful not to trip over the miles of hoses that were laid across the road or not to be run down by an emergency vehicle, but the damned fools were running nonetheless, locked into a regimen of exercise that defied nature's violence.

Floods don't stop them either. They slosh through drenching tropical rains like messengers of Zeus, oblivious to the calamity around them, hearing only the rhythms and the voices that emerge from the headset radios clamped against their ears, their Nikes slapping on the wet pavement, their gazes locked on a distant heaven where fat does not exist and the physically fit are doubly blessed. Amen.

BICYCLES ARE ALSO gaining popularity among aficionados of good health, but since there are damned few places where you can ride them in L.A. and not end up as someone's hood ornament, the number of people using bikes is nowhere close to the number of people running. Unlike Amsterdam, where they have learned to coexist, and Nairobi, where there is hardly any motor vehicle traffic, bicyclists in L.A. take their lives in their hands trying to mingle with the traffic that zooms along our city streets. The little skullcap crash helmets they wear like yarmulkes are about as useless as tits on a bull, as Stepdaddy used to say, when their two-wheeler tangles with a Porsche Targa doing 75 on Malibu Canyon Boulevard.

Bicycling is less, well, spiritual than running, requiring as it does a reasonably alert attitude for those who do not want to end up dead or, worse, unable to ever bicycle again. Its devotees, however, are equally dedicated. A bicyclist–engineering student at UCLA lobbied the city for years to build an overhead freeway exclusively for bicycles, stretching from Westwood over Wilshire Boulevard into Beverly Hills. But since nothing important ever comes out of UCLA except basketball, no one paid his idea much heed and it remains on the drawing board. Bicycle lanes are offered instead, but since a white line on the pavement provides no protection against the automotive tonnage zooming down the road next to you, bicyclists take their lives in their hands when they use them. I think I'd rather skateboard on the freeway than use a bicycle lane.

I WAS HAVING breakfast with my dog one day. He was eating from his bowl on the floor and I was eating from a dish on the table. He was consuming a meaty concoction mixed with chunks of bread and enjoying it immensely. On the other hand, everything I was eating was ersatz. I had substitute eggs and a tofu meat patty. My coffee was an acid-free decaf sweetened with artificial sugar. My cream was nondairy soy milk. Even the salt was a sodium-free "seasoning." Nothing was what it seemed.

I mention that only to point out how much we are into healthy eating in the City of Angles. Vegetarian restaurants and health-food stores are popping up like alfalfa sprouts in hell, and L.A. is eating them up. Vegetarianism has become hip, which implies an aggressive tendency toward proselytizing that is religious in its zeal. Vegetarians are out there converting nonbelievers with the same lofty dedication of missionaries tromping through the jungles of the Mato Grosso looking for souls to save.

We are already accustomed in L.A. to fights based upon cigarette smoking in public places, and now we are nearing the time when otherwise cultured and dignified people will roll on the floor in combat over whether or not the eating of meat ought to be allowed in restaurants. I give you one example of a personal confrontation.

Cinelli and I were in a restaurant with a couple we had just met and the waiter was extolling the virtues of their finest entrée, which was chicken cacciatore. Speaking drama-school Italian American, he said the chicken was so fresh and tender he had eaten it him-a-self that very night. We all said, okay, we'd give it a try, except for the woman, whose name, so help me, was Honey. She said stiffly, "I don't partake of flesh."

I thought she was kidding at first and replied, "We aren't advocating cannibalism here," but, without changing her expression, she said, "I don't partake of any animal flesh." I should have known that anyone who used the Biblical partake and who looked as though she were presiding at an auto-da-fé had no capacity for humor.

"Honey is a vegetarian," her husband, Mac, explained uneasily, clinging to his Scotch and water so hard I thought the glass would break.

"I would prefer that no one partook of flesh at this table," Honey said with great finality.

Cinelli is an accommodating person who tries to avoid trouble whenever possible and ordered rigatoni with a nonmeat sauce. I, on the other hand, suffer fools poorly and informed the waiter as loudly as I could that I would partake of the chicken flesh. Then I added, as cheerfully as possible, "Could you kill it at the table?"

Honey got the message and jerked Mac up off his chair like he was a dog on the couch and off they went. The waiter, who had been silent during the ordeal, said, "I'm-a-sorry, *signore,* we don't-a-kill a-chickens at the table."

I DON'T GIVE a rat's ass what anyone tells you, beauty is the reason for all the health and fitness, but our concept of beauty may be changing. In L.A., we are always looking for the inner person, which is why Eastern religions are so popular here; divine lights will guide us to our murky souls. As a result, we have become a little more tolerant of fat people, whose obesity, of course, is exterior. You will notice their appearance in film and on television to a greater extent than in the past. People like Roseanne, Charles Durning, and the late

John Candy made being fat an asset, and gave permission for others to be fat, too, except for gay men, who are always trim and beautiful. You will never see a fat homosexual in L.A.

What leads me to the hypothesis that fat is becoming more acceptable is the growing number of fat activists in L.A. I became aware of this one day when I attended a convention of the National Association to Advance Fat Acceptance, called to plan new strategy against "size discrimination." They were attempting to rally America's 70 million fat people. Sally Smith called me in advance. She was executive director of NAAFA. I agreed to meet her in a hotel lobby and asked how I'd recognize her. "I'm fat and I have auburn hair," she said.

When I got there, the lobby was loaded with fat women, and many seemed to have auburn hair. But Sally found me. I told her I was short and looked like Albert Einstein. I am short and proud. Fat people, I learned, like to be called fat. Forget euphemisms like chunky or pudgy or overweight. "We prefer being referred to as fat for the same reason blacks prefer being called blacks," she said. " 'Overweight' implies an arbitrary standard, and 'obesity' sounds like a disease. We're fat. Period."

Sally told me that fat people were being fired from jobs because of their size and not their qualifications. "Even worse," she said, "we just heard that in Detroit, a woman who weighed 320 pounds was shot by her sister for being fat and for having asthma."

"That's excessive," I said, for lack of a better response.

"Indeed," Sally said, wondering just how I had intended the comment.

"What I mean is, I wonder whether she was shot for being fat or for having asthma?"

Sally ignored the question and went on to more horror stories of fat people who were rejected, debased, defiled, beaten, tortured, and murdered because they were fat. Another fat activist had a private campaign against fat jokes. He cited one of the worst: "My mother-in-law is fat, but she eats like a bird . . . a vulture." He mentioned a man who collects fat jokes and was willing to sell them to

NAAFA for a dollar each. The activist bought them just to get them off the market.

"This is the beginning of the end of fat jokes," he said.

Later, I asked Shortcut Bernstein if he thought that was true. "Hard to say," he said, pondering the matter. "But at least the fat is in the fire."

THIRTEEN

UNTIL I CAME to Los Angeles, I thought the trial of Burton Abbott was probably the most chaotic event I would ever cover. The race for a single telephone when the guilty verdict came in was like the annual mating stampede of wildebeests across the Masai Mara. There must have been a dozen reporters running to get to that phone, including people from newspapers and wire services that no longer exist, and each of us was determined to be there first, to break the news of Abbott's conviction before anyone else.

A part-time student at UC-Berkeley, Abbott had killed a little girl named Stephanie Bryan, and the emotional urge to see him in hell was a palpable presence in the San Francisco Bay Area of the 1950s, even among members of the press. There was a psychological motive for wanting to be first to break the news, as though we were an integral part of Abbott's condemnation, adding a dangerous new emotional level to the surge to reach that one phone.

The rule of the game was that the phone could not be tied up in advance, so it was every man for himself, the race belonged to the swift, and others clichés popular at the time. Strong men were knocked to the ground, cursing filled the air and fistfights broke out as we elbowed our way out of the courtroom door and down a hall that was probably a hundred feet long, at the end of which the telephone waited, like a virgin goddess ready for ritual deflowering.

I'm not sure who reached the phone first, or if anyone ever got to make the call; perhaps the equipment was ripped from the wall in the chaos and we had to find other means to communicate Abbott's conviction to our city desks. I emerged dazed, battered, and with a sprained back, not quite believing that grown men could react with such frenzy to a single news event. While the conviction of Abbott, who subsequently died in the San Quentin gas chamber, was certainly news, it didn't seem to require such savage response. I said to myself at the time I probably would never see this kind of media stampede again. Then I came to L.A.

Nothing could have prepared me for the media stampedes down here. Imagine wild elephants running amok. Imagine ten thousand Japanese fleeing through the streets of Tokyo with Godzilla gaining on them. Imagine a legion of horny Roman soldiers in hot pursuit of the Sabine women. Imagine a combined New York and Boston Marathon where all of the participants are serial killers. There you've got your L.A. media stampede.

We are not only the nation's second-largest media market, we are the home of celebrity-starved paparazzi, innumerable video freelancers, and more straight media organizations than anyone could possibly imagine. By latest count, there are about seventy newspapers in L.A. County, from the *Valley Acorn* to the *Westchester Journal*. There are also twenty-three wire services, fifty-seven radio stations, twenty-four television stations, and enough magazine reporters, foreign correspondents, and quick-hit authors to fill anyone's nightmare. Put them together with violence and a celebrity and you've got, what else, the O.J. Case.

While I haven't calculated the column inches or timed the number of hours it was on the air, I think I can safely say that the arrest and trial of O.J. Simpson for the murder of Nicole Brown Simpson and Ron Goldman received more national media time and space than any other L.A. crime story in the past fifty years, including both the Manson Family murders and the media avalanche that covered Heidi Fleiss. Part of that is because there's just a lot more media now than there was when Charlie and his kids were killing people, but it is also because the O.J. case involved all the aspects of audience appeal I was talking about earlier.

Nothing, not earthquakes, wars, or landing men on the moon, seemed more important in L.A. than the trial of America's sweet-smiling, wife-beating Monday Night Hero. Newspapers, magazines, radio, tabloids, and television were never without an O.J. story. One television station and one radio station in L.A. ran the trial from gavel to gavel every day it was in session, and the others offered more updates than they did in World War II. They all had legal experts, too, commenting on every aspect of the trial, from Marcia Clark's dating choices to F. Lee Bailey's drinking habits.

Temporary steel towers were erected outside the downtown Criminal Courts Building to facilitate television cameras, and there was enough microwave relay equipment around to cook eggs just by throwing them in the air. Crowds pushed through the vendors around the main doorway of the courthouse to catch a glimpse of somebody, *anybody,* associated with the trial, because they were suddenly all celebrities. The trial judge, Lance Ito, had lunch one day in a nearby restaurant called, somewhat appropriately, Epicenter, and it was as though Barbra Streisand had just walked in the door. We all stared, of course, and I stared the hardest for a while, trying to see what he was eating, but I looked away when he began to stare back. He had the kind of expression on his face that said one more look and I'd be held in contempt, although he wasn't doing any of that during a trial which often seemed vaguely out of control. I mean, the lawyers bitched and pissed on one another in open court, jurors dropped like canaries in nerve gas, and the witnesses all seemed so confused you didn't know what to believe.

At the outset of the trial, Ito cautioned the media not to get crazy on its coverage, then made himself available for special interviews with the big-timers, which set the tone for everyone else to cash in on the notoriety. Kato Kaelin, for reasons that escaped me, became a darling of the day, like a peripheral figure in a soap opera that suddenly edges toward center stage, smiling stupidly at his unexpected good fortune. O.J., meanwhile, got so much mail he felt he had to write a book to answer it, although I don't think he made any decisions in it on the hundreds of requests to marry him or sleep with him or God knows to do what else with him.

THE DAY O.J. pleaded not guilty to the double murders was the worst media day of all. TV vans were jammed bumper to bumper for more than a block outside the courthouse, and inside there were so many cameras, microphones, and human information-seekers that it took on the faint aura of a soccer riot. By comparison, the Burton Abbott blitz seemed like a nanny's walk on the beach.

It was chaotic on the first day of the Heidi Fleiss trial, too, when the waifish angel of sex pleaded not guilty to pandering. Operators of both still and video cameras fought one another for position, and reporters taking notes surged toward Heidi as though simply to touch her they would learn all they needed to know about thousand-dollar whores. Participants feared for their lives in the crush. The weaker wildebeests were pushed aside or trampled asunder. Some found themselves jammed against walls, and others were carried along in the surge with their feet off the ground, like twigs in a flood tide.

"It was like being trampled to death," a shaken Heidi said later. "There was a motorcycle parked outside, and the cameramen just knocked it over. Cameras were swooping in under my face. Someone pulled my hair. I was panicked. I thought they were going to pull my clothes off." They didn't have the same shot at O.J. because he was in custody from the time he stepped out of his white Ford Bronco into the arms of a dozen cops until his acquittal, but you can bet your mama's underwear it would have been worse with him had the cameras been allowed in closer. While football may not be more popular than sex, its heroes are easier to idolize.

Most reporters and news editors justified the mob scenes in both the Heidi and O.J. trials as the legitimate pursuit of interesting if not historic stories. Even Heidi herself had observed with a lopsided smile that "sex sells," though a female reporter for CBS, carried along by the media mob at the courthouse blitz, was heard to say, "I feel so cheap." An NBC television reporter observed during the chaos surrounding O.J., "All the worst clichés about media behavior came true today." Indeed.

Even in her $1.6 million Benedict Canyon home, little Heidi wasn't safe. The paparazzi haunted the place, news helicopters circled overhead, and her four-line telephone rang endlessly. Photographers wildly pursued anyone who entered or left her house, whether it was a friend dropping by to offer moral support or a man delivering pizza. Her lawyer complained that she was a prisoner in her own home, and few would argue with him. O.J. had more privacy because he was in the slammer, although anyone remotely associated with the case was hounded so incessantly they feared for both their safety and their sanity. Especially shaken by excessive media attention was housekeeper Rosa Lopez, who worked for a family near O.J.'s Brentwood home and was in demand as a witness. She was so terrified by the armies of reporters and photographers that descended on her, we all thought Ito would have to tie her to a tree to keep her from sneaking back to El Salvador before she testified. When she finally did take the witness stand, it was anticlimactic, and, having said her piece, she faded into the great, cosmic scheme of things.

BEYOND THE MEDIA storms generated by such as O.J., Heidi, the riots, and other Southern California calamities, nothing makes news like the newsmakers. Our chief fascination is with the doings of local television anchors, those proud but simple people who, eyes glittering with wonder and bewilderment, read us the day's news in varying degrees of fluency. Those with the best eyesight are, if not Ciceronian, at least fluid, because they can read the electronic prompters best.

Local anchors range from a giggling gang of kid co-anchorlings on two competing morning shows (Shortcut Bernstein calls them News Muppets) to solid, no-nonsense performances by grownups in the evening, for which real news is saved that is beyond the ken of the A.M. teens. But even the evening anchors are little more than attractive faces and appealing voices. Don't take my word for it, listen to Howard Rosenberg, the *L.A. Times'* acerbic, Pulitzer Prize–winning television columnist, as he discusses one local anchor:

"He's an impressive package: attractive guy, wears a suit well, communicates facilely, reads a nice story, looks intelligent, has a sense of humor, makes good small talk, and so on and so on. These, not reporting skills or any other kind of journalism pedigree, are the only qualities a local anchor requires. Being smart or perceptive is allowed, if you really must, but it's not a prerequisite. . . . Local anchors rarely face a challenge greater than negotiating their latest contract or reading from a TelePrompTer." He adds: "But who needs *reporters* reading the news anyway?"

Typical of our local anchors and the channel-hopping they engage in is Paul Moyer, who left KABC for KNBC, because it offered him in excess of $8 million for six years, a record amount up until then for a local anchor in any market, even in L.A. He brings to the tube not only those skills mentioned by Rosenberg, but also a child's expression of wonderment that appeals to those who see the world through children's eyes anyhow.

Cinelli doesn't buy his boy-face innocence. She believes his expression is full of subdued malice and his eyes aglitter with a predator's hungry gleam. She would not like to meet him at a watering hole in the jungle. "He will leap from the bush," she says, "his eyes shining and his teeth all white and shiny, and I will hear that terrible melodious voice saying 'This just in . . .' "

Moyer's move from one station to another is not news in a town that can hardly keep up with who is anchoring where. He went where the money was, despite an observation that change is not easy for him. He tends to "snuggle in a place," he says, and "get very comfortable with the people." Now he will have to snuggle up to $8 million, which ought to bring new light to his glittery eyes. Whether or not audiences will flock to his new location remains to be seen. I know Cinelli won't.

We run the full range of anchorism in L.A., the newest element of which is morning news as fun. It's more gang-anchoring than co-anchoring, I guess, in the sense that a bunch of kids have gotten together to deliver the news. They are young and they are happy and reflect those qualities with a good deal of giggling and joshing during periods between segments involving carnage in Rwanda and savagery in Mmabatho. Next to this Brady Bunch of Morning News, even Moyer comes off as mature and competent.

Young and perky aren't the only qualities that have intruded into the television news biz. Try the stand-up anchors at KCOP. They're not bad communicators as TV communicators go, but they roam around the newsroom while reporting the day's events, as though they can hardly wait to get out of the place. "Where the hell are they going?" Shortcut asks rhetorically. I asked that of a KCOP reporter, who said a lot of people wondered the same thing. It gives the impression, one supposes, of anchors on the go, restlessly selling the news, pacing to the grimness it portends. Makes you wanna cry.

DESPITE THE SIZE of Paul Moyer's new paycheck, he was not the big news in town when it came to local anchors. That honor would have to go to Bree Walker and Jim Lampley, who, as co-anchors for KCBS, fell in love right there before our very eyes. It was an on-camera situation matched only by the scene in the movie *The Howling* where the anchorwoman becomes a werewolf on the air and her friend shoots her.

Try as they might, Lampley, a clean-cut guy with a shoe clerk's face, and Walker, blond and doe-eyed, could not hide the chemistry bubbling between them. Howard Rosenberg saw it as coochy-cooing on the eleven o'clock news, while Cinelli regarded it as electronic sex. Either way, the attraction was obviously not just the kind of short-lived professional warmth you might see between, say, a Dan Rather and a Connie Chung. There was heat there, man, and we watched it with fascination, even before the rumor mill began to grind out semiofficial word of the budding relationship. It was the city's most visible office romance.

The fact that both Lampley, forty, and Walker, thirty-six, were married to other people didn't seem to detract at all from the made-for-television love story. Off-camera, they held hands in the hallway and stole kisses in the parking lot and appeared arm in arm at the

L.A. Emmy Awards, all of which filled the plates of those in the media who feed on the rutting habits of celebrities.

Somewhere in the breathless days of their romance, they got divorced from their earlier spouses. Shortly thereafter, KCBS, acknowledging the widespread interest in their relationship, issued a terse announcement: "KCBS-TV is pleased to announce that *Action News* anchors Bree Walker and Jim Lampley will be married in April. No interviews will be granted." Six months later, the couple was wed in the sumptuous private elegance of the seaside Ritz-Carlton Hotel, with only family and close friends in attendance. We dutifully reported that the bride carried an all-white bouquet of lilacs, freesias, and tulips, and that the wedding party lunched on Norwegian salmon.

But wait. The story doesn't end there. Rumors stuck to the newlyweds like drool to a baby. There were reports that the couple had separated, that Lampley was screwing around with other women, and that Walker, in a rage, had tried to run him down in the KCBS parking lot where once they had kissed in the moonlight. Both vociferously denied the rumors. Lampley called the gossip "an uncontrollable rat's nest." Walker attributed it to ambitious colleagues or jealous competitors. Then she had a baby.

Wait again. The story doesn't end there either. Two years after their marriage, KCBS dumped Lampley as anchor. No matter. He had begun as a sports reporter and would go back to sports reporting in a big way at about triple the salary. The management team that had moved him from sports to news anchoring was gone, and the team that replaced it moved Lampley out. He remained at KCBS for a short stint and then moved to NBC, where he's famous and successful doing sports and not hankering for news anchoring anymore. Walker left KCBS, too, and disappeared in limboland. To the best of my knowledge, they're still married and happy and living in Hollywood. Kiss, freeze frame, roll the credits, and fade out.

WHEN IT COMES to print media, the *L.A. by God Times* is the big dog in town. The *Daily News* is a puppy trailing far behind, and anything else of any importance seems small and far away. That is not to say we are necessarily the best thing that ever happened to daily journalism, despite the twenty Pulitzers hanging from our walls; we just happen to be the biggest in Southern California and damned near everywhere else.

It's a different newspaper than the one I joined twenty-three years ago. We are no longer the velvet coffin, in which easy first-class travel was a way of life and bonuses grew with expected annual regularity, like peaches on a tree. We are tougher, tighter, gaudier, more streamlined, less generous, probably younger, and, God help us, politically correct. No matter what they're saying on the street, for example, a woman with spectacular physical attributes is not a babe in the *Times*. An older woman cannot be a biddy. A woman in college is not a co-ed. There is no such thing in our newspaper as a Dutch treat; it is listed in our "Guidelines on Ethnic, Racial, Sexual, and Other Identification" packet as "an offensive reference to sharing expenses."

It is similarly not advisable to say divorcée, gal, hick, holy roller, mankind, man-made, manpower, Indian giver, welsher, hillbilly, or gypped (as in Gypsy), and didn't you know that "French letter" is an offensive reference to condom? If I'd have known it, I'd have used it before it was outlawed. But now that we have become more, well, sensitive, I would not dream of referring to the devise you are slipping over your lower appendage as a French letter. I don't know what I'd call it. I'm afraid to speculate.

All of this came about with the arrival a few years ago of Shelby Coffey III, who replaced Bill Thomas as editor. The younger and more hip SC3 brought with him a nineties feel to a newspaper that was still trying to figure out how to become *The New York Times* of the West. He has made it L.A.'s newspaper without a doubt, but whether that's better or worse than our earlier ambitions remains to be seen. But, what the hell, it's different, and God knows we couldn't go on forever being as drab as chicken potpie. We needed flash and we got it. At least, no one's going to mistake us for the West Coast version of *The New York Times* anymore. We're a nun in bikini underwear.

A lanky, soft-spoken Virginian, Coffey began his career as a sports-writer with the *Washington Post* and became editor of the *L.A. Times* in 1989 at the age of forty-two. He won the job over half a dozen other contenders when then publisher Tom Johnson asked them all to write essays on why they wanted to be editor, a step upward from "What I Did on My Vacation," but in the same general manner. The idea provided a lot of laughs for people in the business, but it helped get Coffey the editorship. That's more than I've ever gotten for writing essays.

I met Coffey in person before he'd had much of a chance to warm his new chair. I'd been kicking around the Valley as a columnist for the suburban editions and wanted to go downtown full-run instead of appearing only in special sections. Timing was everything here. I'd just won a couple of national awards and was being offered jobs elsewhere, so I took all that to Coffey and ended up in the full-run Metro section.

Not that it has been caviar and Diet Coke ever since, as Irving Wallace used to say. Coffey decided at some point that all the Metro columns ought to be 80 percent reportage and 20 percent "embroidery," which we took to mean our personal opinions. Up until then, I was writing a lot of whimsy and humor mostly off the top of my head but with, say, 23.5 percent reportage; in other words, heavy on the embroidery. I was advised that all of this had to change and was subsequently cut from three to two columns a week to see if I would concentrate more on reportage. "To give me more time for research" was the way they put it. But like a pit bull with his teeth clamped on a mailman's ass, I'm dedicated to my muse and manage at least 22 percent embroidery most of the time. Once I went 26 percent. They let it go.

I should have known this was coming. When I first met Shelby he suggested I do more repor-*tage,* with a French pronunciation, and fewer columns that contained bodily humor. I hadn't been aware of doing a lot of scatology, except for the piece on Zeke the Do-Do King and maybe a few others, but I said okay. Clearly, Coffey wanted something different than what I was doing, although the senior editor, who was Noel Greenwood at the time, said to just keep doing what I was doing. It was after that they chopped me down to two columns a week.

I don't argue with SC3. For one thing, it has been my policy for many years to avoid editors as often as possible, and also because during his watch the paper's Metro staff has won two Pulitzers for coverage of the '92 riots and the '94 earthquake, so he must be doing everything right. We were also a finalist for coverage of the '93 wildfires, and we're set to go again should Malibu drop off into the sea or Beverly Hills go broke.

I'm pretty happy at what I'm doing, except that everybody gets a little tense when I write about sex. That doesn't surprise me. Newspapers, unless they're tabloids, have always been afraid of sex. We have not come far from the days of the *Oakland Tribune* when a managing editor ordered the testicles airbrushed off the photo of a bull, and, later, the navel airbrushed from the picture of a woman in a swimsuit. "There'll be no smut in this journal," I recall him saying. Those were the days when smut was the target of every Jesus-loving, psalm-singing son of a bitch who came down the pike. It hasn't changed much.

A lot of newspaper editors are still like the woman who fainted every time a sexual term was used. It was a famous court case. I forget the name of the mental pathology, but she claimed she had been raped by a man who knew she suffered from the malady and who said dirty words to keep her unconscious while he did it to her. She keeled over a couple of times in court when sexual references were made, just to prove her point. The guy was convicted.

Similarly, newspapers have almost made writing sex in a crowded newsroom a crime similar to shouting fire in a crowded theater. But after twelve years of writing a column for America's biggest family newspaper, I know it works. Anytime I want to see an editor crumble, I whisper *genitalia* and down he goes.

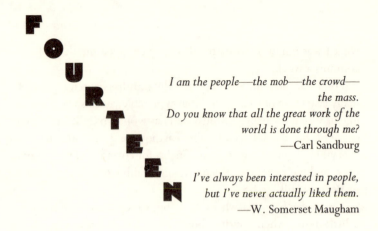

*I am the people—the mob—the crowd—
the mass.
Do you know that all the great work of the
world is done through me?*
—Carl Sandburg

*I've always been interested in people,
but I've never actually liked them.*
—W. Somerset Maugham

NOT EVERYONE IN L.A. is in show biz. In addition to actors, writers, directors, and others we refer to as being above-the-line, we are also shoe clerks, air-conditioning repairmen, freeway litter removers, popcorn salesmen, female mud wrestlers, and the creators of logos that appear on T-shirts. This is by way of saying we are a heterogeneous mix in the nation of Los Angeles, and it is my job as a newspaper columnist to write about the mélange. Actors are simply a part of the mix, but like blueberries in a muffin, they happen to be more obvious.

Take Wayne Rogers. He came by one day after *M.A.S.H.* had gone off the air to prep for a series that involved newspaper reporters. Like Randy Quaid, Ed Asner, and some others I can't remember, actors about to portray journalists spend a day or so hanging around the newsroom, hoping to soak up some of the wit and wisdom traditionally associated with our workplaces. They often leave disappointed after determining that being wise and witty isn't prerequisite to working on a newspaper. Being able to type and hold your liquor is.

After Rogers looked around the *Times* for a while, I took him to lunch across the street at the Red Dog, a hangout for reporters, lawyers, cops, and amateur hookers. As it turned out, I don't remember eating at all because Rogers was instantly recognized by women in the place who began sending over drinks in hopes, I suppose, of being the one he took home. That's what I mean by actors being more obvious. Every time they sent a drink over to him, they included the table, which included me, though they expressed no desire for me to take them home.

Hours later I staggered out of the Red Dog, leaving Rogers and a television writer to fend for themselves and to make of our business what they would, not really giving a damn what anyone thought. I returned to the city room, bounced off the walls for a while, and was finally driven home by co-workers who did not want to see me perish on the Hollywood Freeway, although the symbolism must have been tempting. As an editor observed back then, they carried me out on my shield. Whatever series Rogers was interested in never got off the ground.

It was after that that Ed Asner came around to research his role as city editor in the *Lou Grant* series, for which I became technical adviser the first season. We adjourned once more to the Red Dog, but a few years had passed since the Wayne Rogers debacle and I was no longer interested in trying to drink the room under the table. A group of us simply did our best to infuse Asner with all the attributes of a great, socially minded city editor. We did so well that eventually he began to think of himself that way and tried to save the world. But it isn't the role of an actor or a city editor to save anything. That's up to community activists.

I'VE NEVER SEEN a place where so many people objected to so many things in forums of public opinion. There are eighty-eight cities in L.A. County and every one of them has a half-dozen or so activists who keep things in a state of chaos. When I say activists, I don't mean those of a temperate nature who meet over butter cookies and decaffeinated coffee to discuss the need for a neighborhood litter committee on Lullaby Lane.

We are talking here about a snarling breed of mad-dog, kamikaze protesters who rage at public meetings, yell at civic leaders, battle cops, eat live chickens, chain themselves to historic buildings, throw themselves in the path of bulldozers, and generally let it be known that they'd rather die than surrender.

They oppose sewer systems, sex shops, airport noise, churches, bus routes, road closures, road openings, bars, expansion, demolition, jails, medical facilities, libraries, industry, whorehouses, and dogs that bark after nine o'clock at night. That's on a community level. Some of them graduate to oppose war, hunger, homelessness, political oppression, disease, child abuse, red meat, environmental pollution, food additives, water impurities, police violence, sexual harrassment, cigarette smoke, and spousal abuse.

A good example of the aforementioned were the two Jerry Rubins of L.A., who represented activism in most of its various forms. Rubin One was the famous Rubin, the screaming yippie who terrorized the Establishment twenty-five years ago and went on to become a member of the Chicago 7. When I met him, he was into the network marketing of various health powders, including an orange-flavored drink called Wow! Rubin Two was a local activist who had alternately benefited and suffered from having the same name as the more famous Rubin. He was still a peace activist, but because peace had fallen on hard times, he had been forced to take a job potting orchids for six dollars an hour.

I had known Rubin Two for many years. He lived on the beach at Venice and was L.A. director of Alliance for Survival, which was how he made his living. He took half of the profits from the Alliance's antiwar activities and managed to struggle by on about six thousand dollars a year. When the Berlin Wall came down and Russia fell apart, so did L.A.'s interest in antiwar functions. As a result, Rubin Two, with only two dollars in the bank, had to start looking for another way to support himself. I wrote about his dilemma, and that's when Rubin One came into the picture.

He was in my face before you could chant "Hey, hey, LBJ, how many babies have you killed today?" and was relentless in his demand for what he called a clarification column. He wanted me to explain it was the Other Jerry Rubin and not him, the Famous Jerry Rubin, who was on his ass. "Women won't go out with me because they think I only have two dollars to my name and where the hell could I take them with two dollars?" he said in a barrage of words that whistled past my ear like .50-caliber bullets.

I ignored him as long as I could, despite his endless phone calls, but when he had his friends, his ex-wife, his lawyer, and even Rubin Two call to beg for a clarification column, I figured I would either do a follow-up or be driven mad by the man and his equally determined compatriots. It was a small taste of what he did to everyone back in the 1960s, when they finally ended the Vietnam War just to shut him up. Lyndon Johnson, it is said, declined to run for a second term to get out of his line of fire.

I got the two Rubins together in Number One's $5,000-a-month high-rise apartment on the west side of L.A. I expected to see a fight to the death, like two pit bulls going at each other, but instead Rubin One dominated the conversation, trying to induce Rubin Two into giving up his orchid-potting job for the sake of pride in their common name and let him, Rubin One, make Rubin Two rich selling Wow! and other vitamin-rich powders. R-Two politely declined and remained quiet most of the time, listening to the Other Rubin talk about his fame and wealth and place in history and the pathetic financial state of R-Two. Potting orchids, indeed!

Rubin Two wasn't usually that docile. He'd been in jail a few times for challenging the Establishment and was famous for having thrown a pie in the face of physicist Edward Teller, so-called Father of the H-bomb. He could be a wild man in pursuit of a cause and dominated the local activist scene, whether it was fighting to get toy guns off the market or trying to maintain the ambience of the Venice Boardwalk. He could rant and rave and wave his fist along with the best of them and was known for his prolonged fasts. No face was more familiar in L.A. than the face of Jerry Rubin Two staring out from a television screen, his expression twisted into indignant outrage and his eyes wide with incredulity, ready to hurl himself into hell for a heavenly cause.

Rubin One, the famous Rubin, the yippie Rubin, kept after

R-Two but they never got together again after that one meeting. The man who had once defied the government of the United States and who later defied the very principles he once held dear, defied a red light while crossing Wilshire Boulevard a few months later and was struck by a car. He lay in the street like a fallen flag and died without ever regaining consciousness. Even in death, there was the kind of confusion he'd tried to avoid. The friends of Rubin Two, the Venice Rubin, thought he was the one who'd been killed, and sent messages of condolence to his wife.

THERE ARE ALMOST as many community activists in L.A. as there are actors. To name a few more, there's a guy who pulled down his pants and mooned a suburban city council in a dispute over population growth and who maintained later it was not a full moon but only a quarter moon; the two women activists who got into a fistfight at a local city hall and thrashed and rolled through the corridors for several minutes before they could be separated; and the cowboy who rode his horse into a civic meeting in order to make a point about preserving rural areas.

They are usually physically ejected from the meetings and sometimes are forced to cool off behind bars. Occasionally, one of them ends up in a straitjacket or shackled to a bed in the psycho ward of the county hospital. But at least it keeps them in the news, which is their ultimate goal.

However, I do not mean to imply that we are all activists, although it seems that way sometimes, due to the fire and smoke that hellraisers manage to create. Actors and activists occupy a common niche in their mutual efforts to be noticed. But lost in the shuffle of pretty faces and loud voices is the rest of L.A., and it is of them I sing the most. People like Ellyn Windsor.

She was a bright, plumpish woman of fifty-one who lived alone in a condo on the edge of upscale Bel-Air. On the day I met her, she was one of 2,701 patients in the U.S. waiting for a donor heart. Two massive coronaries had left her with only 30 percent of her heart functioning. Her father had died of a heart attack at age fifty-four, and by smoking four packs of cigarettes a day for twenty-five years, Ellyn Windsor was chasing his ghost to the grave.

After her second attack, the head of UCLA Medical Center's transplant unit suggested they discuss a transplant. Windsor was incredulous. "Are you crazy?" she demanded. "Transplants are for flowers and trees, not for me." Her cardiologist broke it as gently as he could in a room where time seemed suspended in an awesome silence. He said, "It's the only way you're going to live."

Thereafter, she became a woman obsessed with living, afraid to wander too far from the area of the hospital that would save her life, waiting for the phone to ring to tell her the time had come. A professional fund-raiser, she curtailed her activities sharply to preserve what energy she had for the ordeal ahead, but this too became a burden. Alone and idle, it gave Windsor time to load herself with guilt, knowing that someone had to die for her to live; perhaps a young person who had known life for such a little while. . . .

Then one day the telephone rang. A voice said, "This is the UCLA Medical Center transplant coordinator. We have a heart for you." The time had come. Six months in a twilight world, suspended between life and death, were nearing an end. Soon, a stranger's heart would beat in her chest. Soon, the terrible waiting would be over. But it was not to be. After examining the heart that was to be Windsor's, they discovered the donor had hepatitis-B. The transplant was off. They sent her home.

I thought about Windsor many times after that. She had promised me she would call when the time came again. I would be part of her routine: She would call her son, her daughter, a friend to drive her, and me. My column had made her a kind of local celebrity; it had given her a moment in the sun. Many waited with Ellyn Windsor.

I returned late from work one night. The red light of my answering machine was blinking. It was Windsor's voice, filled with excitement and good cheer. "I'm on my way," it said. "Wish me luck!" That would be the last I would ever hear from her. Her son left a message the next day. His mother had died on the operating table. All that waiting, all that hoping, all that anguish, all that fear had perished in her chemically induced sleep. But at least the anguish would die, too.

Her voice, that final message, remained on my machine for weeks thereafter. I found it difficult to erase the last evidence of her life on earth, but eventually I did. I said, "Good-bye, Ellyn," and pushed the button.

FIFTEEN

EVERY YEAR AROUND Thanksgiving, celebrities summon the media, gather at a place of convenience, sit on the floor, and eat rice with their fingers. Well, not all of them. Some eat delicacies prepared by local chefs, and others, those in between the rice-eaters and the gourmands, are served both beans and rice from a communal pot. The idea is to illustrate the imbalance of food distribution in the world, and what better way to do it in L.A. than to amass a group of well-intentioned celebs who are between jobs?

Forget that later the same day a lot of those who ingest the small portions of rice might sneak off to Citrus or L'Hermitage or Ristorante Il Rex to dine on something other than what 60 percent of the world is forced to eat. They reason that someday the poor will have gourmet restaurants of their own and will understand why a star is unable to exist on a handful of rice eaten off of a banana leaf. If God had wanted famous people to eat so poorly, why would he have created *poitrine de veau?*

Even at that banquet to call attention to world hunger, the famous who picked at their meager meal couldn't bring themselves to drink tap water or water from a dirty stream, which is what all those hungry people have to do. They stood in line for cups of water all right, but it was bottled Evian water. That, and the mimicking of starvation by well-heeled people who pay $75 to $150 to attend are among the criticisms heard regarding the airy display of show biz conscience.

Jon Voight, who cohosted one event with Valerie Harper, angrily denounced the media for its harsh and critical ways, then asked, "Why don't those people ever do anything themselves? There are many different ways to pray, and I think that we're gathered here in prayer." Cybill Shepherd prayed at an earlier starvation banquet by posing for pictures on a straw mat surrounded by milk crates and an overturned trash can in order to illustrate living conditions in the Third World. She ate rice with her fingers while cameras rolled and strobe lights popped. I don't know why the milk crates, since I doubt that they have many lying around in, say, Somalia, but maybe that's all they could find to dress the set.

I mention the world hunger affair only to illustrate to what extent celebrities will go in order to support their causes. Dinner without wine is about as primitive as some stars will ever get, though Voight, who fancies himself closer to the people, probably doesn't miss it. I'm not sure about Cybill Shepherd or Valerie Harper or any of the dozens of others who performed by eating, or not eating, at the affair.

I don't mean to impugn the noble intentions of those who forsake lobster ravioli for scant portions of rice. I was asked by an actor friend to join him in starving at the last banquet but was already committed to dining with bail bondsman Joey Barnum and the late ex-con artist Joe Seide at Matteo's, which is the restaurant in town where Frank Sinatra eats when he is up from Palm Springs. Matty Giordano does not serve small portions of rice to his customers. He heaps their plates with huge servings of osso buco and linguine and clams. We go there to eat, to get fat, and to perhaps see Sinatra stroll in. I sat in his booth one night and swear to Our Maker I felt a warm glow coming up from my ass to my heart.

"It's like a religious experience," I said to Cinelli. "I feel like crying."

"Leave it alone," she said.

Celebrities crowd Matteo's every Sunday night. No one knows

exactly why Sunday is such a big deal, but it is. Milton Berle swings by and Phyllis Diller and Henny Youngman and Rodney Dangerfield and other oldtime Hollywoodians. I met Cher's mom there one night and she told me she was celibate.

"Why'd she tell you that?" Cinelli demanded. "Did you proposition her?"

"No way. We were talking about the environment or something and she suddenly said she hadn't been laid for six years."

"She said she hadn't been laid?"

"Well," I said, "she didn't put it that way. I think she said she hadn't been with a man."

"Maybe she meant she had no male friends."

"Maybe. But I think she meant she hadn't been laid."

"You have a way of putting things," she said.

Ronald Reagan used to go to Matteo's before he came down with Alzheimer's disease. Maurice Duke went there, too. Duke is a television producer, who is full of bombast and goodwill. Reagan is a former actor in B-movies. The way Duke tells it, they were there on the same night once. A Sunday, of course.

Duke saw Reagan and shouted, "What're you eating?"

"Huh?" Reagan said, in a reply familiar to millions.

"WHAT'RE YOU EATING?" the Duke shouted even louder.

"Huh?" Reagan said again.

The Duke rose halfway out of his chair, ready to bellow at him a third time, by now determined to learn what the fortieth President of the United States was having for dinner. But Nancy Reagan, forever on the alert, leaned over and whispered in her husband's ear as the room waited in anticipation.

Then a split second before Duke's voice would rattle the chandeliers, the man who led the free world for eight perilous years blinked and replied amiably, "Chicken."

Duke sighed and sat down. The room went back to eating.

THE JEWISH DELICATESSEN Nat 'n' Al's is also a place where famous people go. Everyone calls its regulars the Matzo Ball Mafia. Nat's also does not serve small portions of rice, but stuffs its customers with huge pastrami-on-rye sandwiches, possibly the largest in the world. I mention the place not only because it is the antithesis of a hunger banquet, but because of the presence of the waitress Kaye Coleman. She came up with what may have been The Best Original Line Ever Said by a Waitress while waiting on David Begelman one day. You remember him. He was president of Columbia Pictures, who, at the time, was being investigated for forging checks. When he was finished eating, he asked Kaye if he could sign the tab. Quick as a flash, Kaye says, "You can sign the tab, but I want the tip in cash."

EATING RICE WITH one's fingers is not the only manner by which celebrities support their special causes. In L.A., we have witnessed everything from wet T-shirt contests to black-tie galas. From nipples to napkins, you might say. There have been walks, runs, bicycle rides, motorcycle rides, footraces, water sports, golf tournaments, volleyball tournaments, sand sculpturing, telethons, dances, gambling nights, comedy shows, beach parties, art shows, fashion shows, parades, athletic contests, jazz concerts, barbecues, carnivals, circuses, cake sales, and just plain hanging around to be seen.

The activities are meant to promote, discourage, or somehow benefit dolphins, whales, coyotes, drug abuse, cigarette smoking, homeless children, AIDS, handgun control, open space, cancer research, domestic pets, vegetarianism, cystic fibrosis, lupus erythematosus, muscular dystrophy, earth pollution, Alzheimer's disease, abortion rights, lung diseases, heart diseases, various diseases of the poor, the environment, food purity, Indian rights, male impotence, immigrant rights, various groups of ethnic boat people, animal spaying and neutering, saving the rain forest, alternative transportation, mosquito abatement, senior health, farm workers' rights, nuclear hazards, the ocean, freedom of the arts, the rights of the physically, mentally, and culturally challenged, the emotional, sexual, and economic abuse of women, and gang control, to name one or two.

Once committed to a cause, no group is more determined than those in show biz to see that the cause is upheld. Take animals. L.A.

is in the forefront of fighting animal abuse from lab rats to Thanksgiving turkeys, and a good many of those involved in the effort are actors. It is a cause that requires minimal talent and absolutely no ability at abstract logic, which makes it perfect for people in show biz. All you've got to be able to do is hug your doggie and make an occasional appearance at rallies condemning cruelty to polo ponies.

As an example of their fervor, I take you to a kennel in the San Fernando Valley being picketed by members of Last Chance for Animals, an especially, well, rabid group of animal activists. The picketing came to my attention when a woman called to say people with crazy eyes were chanting and looking in her window. She had called the police, but they said there was no law against picketing or having crazy eyes. That's when the poor thing turned to me.

It was my first experience with the animal activists of L.A. They are a scruffy bunch who, by manner and appearance, seem to mimic the dogs whose interests they support. One looked exactly like a Clydesdale terrier, another like a Shetland sheepdog, though not as clean. The woman who telephoned me was caretaker at the kennel, which Last Chance was accusing of accepting animals on the pretense of finding them homes and then selling them to laboratories for research. She had no idea whether or not the owners sold dogs to labs. All she knew was feed the beasts and clean up their doo-doo.

I could not tell by looking at the animals whether or not they were destined for scientific dabbling. There were seventeen dogs, fifteen cats, and six rabbits. The dogs barked, the cats meowed, and the rabbits thumped. Last Chance for Animals was not interested in the rabbits, but then, as I understand it, neither were the laboratories. The rabbits were left to eat and fornicate and be happy. Therein lies a lesson for us all.

The noise in the kennel was deafening. I can't even take the noise of my own dog Hoover, who is old and feeble and whose effort at barking is somewhere between a shout and a yowl. Cinelli thinks he's saying Lowell when he barks. Outside the kennel waited the soldiers of Last Chance for Animals. Also, there was Barbara Fabricant, the widow of Sid the Squid. Barbara is a state humane officer who also dabbles in the occult. Whenever I need a transchannelist or a past-life regressionist, I call Barbara.

She wasn't all that convinced the kennel was selling animals to research centers. As I talked to her I took notes. That's what journalists do. If we don't ask questions and take notes, there is no reason to have us around. In the middle of the interview, a Last Chancer strode toward us and said, "What's going on here?" He was long-haired and unshaven. His voice had the yapping quality of a Pekingese. I learned later he was an unemployed actor.

"I'm interviewing the lady," I said. The hair on the back of my neck stood up.

"About what?" he yapped.

"That's none of your business," I growled.

"I want to know what's going on here!"

He made the mistake of grabbing my notebook. You can grab for a lot of things either attached or unattached to my person. Grab for my money, grab for my nose, grab for my round, preppy Liz Claiborne glasses, or grab for my crotch, and I will let you live, *but never by God never grab for my notebook when I am in the middle of an interview!*

"I will give you about five seconds to return my notebook," I said to the actor, "after which I will plant a midlength Florsheim boot in your balls." There was no mistaking my intent. I meant every word. The actor understood that and reluctantly returned my notebook, thus preserving both his balls and my reputation for basic nonviolence. We observed each other thereafter with naked hostility, much as warring dogs remain enemies from a distance for the length of their association.

I never did find out whether or not the kennel was selling animals to research laboratories, but it really didn't matter. I suggested later in a column that perhaps science ought to consider substituting animal activists for animals in their research, thereby eliminating the need for protest while simultaneously allowing the protesters to become martyrs to their cause. I never heard from Last Chance for Animals, but I did hear from a lot of people who said it was a hell of an idea. That's what comes from grabbing a journalist's notebook.

SHORTCUT BERNSTEIN HAS often pointed out that there are more celebrities looking for causes than there are causes, and someone is going to have to come up with more causes. He suggests that an organization be formed to identify new diseases and social issues that need addressing by famous people, if only for a moment. That seems cynical and inappropriate to me, which is one reason I like Shortcut, but I doubt it will ever come to pass.

However, there are individuals and organizations that put celebrities together with charities and causes in search of higher profiles. A match is made when someone in the entertainment industry, usually on the way up or on the way down, is seeking visibility at about the same time an organization is looking for a spokesperson. One organization works from a list of 2,500 celebrities willing to step before the camera on behalf of a disease or cause of the moment. This is not dissimilar from those organizations that compile lists of psychiatrists willing to testify in court one way or the other on any given issue. The only difference is that a psychiatrist gets money in exchange for his expertise, while a celebrity gets glory in exchange for his face.

Here's how it would work: Say you've got a sudden upsurge in L.A. of cruelty to werewolves. This falls both into the animal-abuse category and perhaps civil rights for the homeless, since werewolves are essentially, well, migratory, and therefore homeless. Werewolves are also essentially male, since various chemicals in the female glandular system protect women against the curse of lycanthropy. This naturally attracts young, recently empowered women who are drawn by both their natural feminine instincts to nurture living creatures and by the image of the werewolf as the ultimate male, savage and free and sexual. Women are attracted to werewolves for the same reason they're attracted to cowboys and drywall plasterers: A small voice within them asks, *Just how would it be to grapple with a beast half-man and half-animal?* Images of multiple orgasms dance in their heads.

Thus motivated, they band together to form the Werewolf Action Group (WAG) and begin looking around for ways to publicize it for the purpose of raising funds. They need a spokesperson who would appropriately represent their cause, someone hairy who drools and growls and isn't too bright. This immediately suggests any number of rock musicians who fit the description to a T. However, an agency that specializes in putting celebrities together with new causes takes a different approach: Go against type. In other words, cast a sweet, sincere young woman as a spokesperson for WAG and feature her, small and vulnerable, holding the hand of a large, howling, red-eyed beast and saying, "Won't you help?" Sally Struthers? Too old. Anna Pacquin? Too young. Winona Ryder? No longer innocent. You need someone named Tina who is pert and sweet and whose breasts do not cascade over the top of her blouse, and who has not been featured in the tabloids for screwing rock drummers.

You get the idea. Somewhere out there there's a woman who fits the classic image of the beauty in love (innocently) with the beast, and whose message for money will claw at your heart, metaphorically speaking. At the end of her message, which will fairly ooze compassion, the werewolf will stop his howling, cease his growling, turn his mad, red, killer eyes toward her and, for a moment, smile. Then he will become human again and everyone will clap. Pan toward the full moon, freeze frame, and fade out.

SIXTEEN

SPRING 1995. It is a peaceful Saturday in L.A. The sky is blue following a few days of welcomed light rain. Green grass and wildflowers are growing amid the chaparral once blackened by brushfires. Rock and mud slides triggered by our most recent storms have been cleared from Malibu Canyon and Pacific Coast Highway. There were no ATM murders last night and there hasn't been a drive-by killing in a week. Peace prevails like the music of lutes over a city at play in the sunshine . . . and I don't trust it.

It makes me nervous, all this quiet. It is not like the Los Angeles I have come to know and endure and fear in the past few years. Too much tranquillity, as Shortcut is prone to point out, dulls the senses. An eland at peace cannot detect a lion with the same quickness as an eland on the alert. I am more accustomed to a city whose festivals traditionally go to hell. Take, for instance, a recent Cinco de Mayo celebration.

We called it Fiesta Broadway so as not to make it too, you know, ethnic, but its real purpose was to acknowledge Mexico's victory over France in the Battle of Puebla in 1862. (For detailed information, visit your local library or ask a smart Mexican.) To accommodate the fiesta, we cordoned off forty square blocks in the downtown area and filled it for a weekend with booths and music and several hundred thousand people. This was the fifth annual fiesta. Four others had gone by without incident. But L.A. was not under the influence of angry gods back then.

I went to the latest fiesta on a Sunday. Cinelli was with me. We wandered from Spring Street, which is the home of the *L.A. by God Times,* to Broadway, a stroll of about two blocks to the center of the celebration. There we were confronted with a sight to gladden the open, waiting hearts of every multiculturalist in America: white people and brown people and black people and yellow people mixing in dedicated amiability in the core of a city not known recently for either its urban euphoria or its joie de vivre.

"Now *this* is more like the L.A. we came to twenty years ago," Cinelli said. "People having a good time without the necessity of firing their AK-21s in the air or gang-raping their neighbors."

"I think they're AK-47s," I said, "but I like the way you put that."

"It's true. Conviviality is everywhere. Look at that mother and her little girl, running toward us laughing. Look at all those young people . . . running toward us and shouting. Look at all those men . . . why does everyone seem to be running toward us?"

"To begin with," I said, pushing her into an open doorway, "that mother and daughter aren't laughing, they're crying. That is fact number one. Fact number two is, if you peer into the distance, you will see skirmish lines of policemen in riot gear, their batons at the ready, trotting forward behind them, causing them all to run."

"Well," Cinelli said with a long sigh, "there goes the party."

Indeed. No one seems to know even now exactly what happened. Either there was trouble or the smell of trouble when the performance of a rock group was canceled on a stage set up on the street farther down Broadway. It is easier to start a riot in L.A. by canceling or overselling a rock concert than by overthrowing the mayor. While the precise flash point of chaos remains in doubt, everyone agrees there was a lot of shouting and cursing, either of which was enough to trigger a police presence. Dozens of cops in face masks and helmets came marching in like troops from a Darth Vader army, at which point, as we like to say, the shit hit the fan.

What Cinelli and I were seeing was the result of all that had transpired around the stage. Suddenly, there were cops everywhere and helicopters overhead and patrol cars pushing their way through the crowds on the periphery and bullhorns that warned everyone to disperse. We were in the middle of all that. I told Cinelli to stay in the doorway while I draped police press credentials around my neck, but she wanted to see, too, so off we marched into the Valley of Death.

Rocks and bottles sailed over our heads with the grace of birds on the wing, and I swear to God several of the policemen were zeroing in on me as the person they would beat first if given half a chance. The LAPD is not known for sane target selection or grants of mercy in times of stress and confusion. The best I could do was get both Cinelli and me the hell out of the way and pray for redemption. Fresh in my mind was the response of a cop who ordered me to move in a similar situation. When I showed him my press credentials, he said I had to move anyhow. When I said, "Suppose I don't"—anticipating perhaps an arrest and legal action—he said, "I'll kick your ass." So I moved.

As it turned out, a few people were arrested, but no one was killed or maimed. Cinelli and I ended up in a nearby restaurant without once having had our asses kicked. Just another day in L.A.

ANOTHER FESTIVAL HAS since passed in relative peace, but the aforementioned still stands as an example of the unexpected calamity that has befallen the City of Angles in the past few years, beginning with the riots. I think we could have taken those okay without feeling cursed and doomed, coming out of them as we did overflowing with love for those less fortunate than we. The feeling lasted, well, for months before we went back to a more sensible brand of selective loving, the category for which did not include anyone who wanted anything from us, whether it was time or money. We loved black old ladies on pension and Latino children whose fathers were not in jail. The homeless can go to hell.

It was good to get back to a more normal mode of life, and for a short while we basked in the lunacy that is L.A. in repose. But then, just a little more than a year later, God tried to burn us down. The fires of autumn 1993 were damned scary, and Cinelli and I were right in the middle of them. They burned up to a quarter of a mile away, which is almost next door when the Santa Ana winds are howling like ladies from Hades in the mountains and coming in your direction.

We had to evacuate overnight, which was okay with me, because I have no desire to be spit-roasted in the twilight of my years. But still, it's an eerie feeling looking back and knowing that your house and everything in it could be a smoldering heap of ashes when you return. I thought about crazy things like the stuffed piranha on a shelf in my writing room that Cinelli bought for me because she said we had similar smiles; and the Purple Hand of God that hangs on a thin wire over my desk and sways when there's an earthquake. Actually, it's a hand from a mannequin that I found in the Garment District and reminds me that sitting at the word processor is where I ought to be most of the time and not out screwing off somewhere.

As it turned out, our house didn't burn. The piranha and I still smile at each other occasionally, and the Purple Hand of God still points downward at my word processor. I obey.

We get fires every few years in L.A., burning through the mountains and hillside that surround the city. They destroy homes and kill people with a kind of fearsome caprice that spares some places and destroys others, and causes traffic jams you wouldn't believe, which really pisses everyone off. But the fires of '93 were somehow different; I'm not sure why. There was something almost spiritual about their blazing against a pure blue sky, with palm trees burning like tiki torches along the beach at Malibu, and sirens contributing contrapuntally to the chaos that accompanies big disasters, and celebrities wandering here and there, causing gasps of disbelief from the firefighters flown in from Utah.   •

There were nineteen fires that season throughout Southern California in a three-week period, which meant that just about everyone was affected. You could see flames at night and smoke during the day, with ashes falling onto both the ghettos of South Central and the wide green lawns of Beverly Hills. No sooner would one wildfire seem to die out than another start. Most were set by arsonists or stupid people, which took a lot of the spirituality out of them but added elements of rage to the terror we all felt. An army of fire-fighters from throughout the country joined our own outmanned forces in confronting flames as high as heaven and finally stopped them, but not until 1,200 homes were burned and three people were dead. Damage totaled a billion dollars.

Because fires are extraordinarily visual and full of noise and drama, every television station in the city covered them continuously, pre-empting even the kind of crapola America usually feeds on, which caused a lot of telephone calls at the stations. Fire or no fire, they wanted their *Days of Our Lives* and their *Roseanne*. I suspect they will feel the same way at the end of the world, wondering in the last ter-rible seconds of existence if there is *Seinfeld* in eternity.

FOLLOWING THE FIRES there was once more a brief period of nothing going on in L.A. except the usual gang killings, religious hustles, white-collar crime, and celebrity whoring. It lasted for a full two months. I amused myself by writing about an ex-madam named Cheri Woods, freshly out of prison, who hired a public relations firm to tell the world how much better a businesswoman she was than Heidi Fleiss. She had given up hooking and was studying to be a real estate broker, which she felt incorporated a lot of the kind of work with which she had become familiar. In L.A., everything seems to boil down to a form of prostitution. It has something to do with the effect of sunlight filtered through smog.

I also wrote about a defrocked Methodist minister who had al-legedly caught his wife in bed with another man, but instead of killing them both, he committed a more tragic deed. He made a movie about it. The man's name is Larry Howard and the movie was called *Four Day Shoot*. You never saw it because it was only in a the-ater once, and he had to rent the place to get it there. The movie cost him $400,000 and was just a little better than the home videos Grandma takes. Howard was a 1960s drug-using hippie who entered the ministry during an acid-induced cosmic epiphany, but was kicked out when he went public with his plan to make *Four Day Shoot*. He made it anyhow, showed it once, and disappeared into the crowds around Hollywood. The last time I saw him, he was thinking about making a film for children.

It was a relief after the wildfires to deal in nothing more important than sex and movies, but it was not to last. The earthquake followed in a few months and then a lot of devastating storms and floods, intermingled with murders and trials and hate crimes and politics . . . and O.J. Simpson.

IT IS ABOUT a year since his epic ninety-mile journey on the freeways of L.A. Simpson was wanted for the murder of his ex-wife and a man who was visiting her. He was to have surrendered at noon, but instead vanished with a friend, Al Cowlings. Their car was spotted in Orange County, and for two hours, their odyssey held us transfixed as television helicopter cameras charted their journey on three different freeways that finally led to his home in the privileged community of Brentwood.

It was surreal. Cowlings drove and for much of the time Simpson held a gun to his head. Only hours before, another friend had made public a note the Hall of Famer had left for him. If it wasn't a suicide note, it came close. We wondered if the former football great would pull the trigger. So help me God, we worried about him. The drama held us entranced. Television never left it. It was prime-time reality. Drivers listening to their radios pulled their cars to a stop along the freeways traveled by Simpson and Cowlings. They waved their support. Some shouted, "Go, Juice!" as though this were a football game, and his zigzag route through traffic was another heart-pounding run.

Men who had played on the same football teams took to the airwaves to urge the forty-six-year-old jock to give up. Others couldn't believe he would do what he was doing. He must have been on drugs. He must have been mad. Men cried and women prayed, and vice versa. It was an American tragedy, some said. The more cynical deflated that. It was, at best, a *football* tragedy, they explained. O.J. was a sports hero, not a statesman. The real tragedy was in the deaths of two human beings. The real tragedy was that Simpson may have stalked and killed his beautiful ex-wife Nicole and her friend Ronald Goldman, although a jury felt otherwise. The tragedy was murder, not the fall from grace of a football icon.

Even after his surrender to police at his tree-shaded Tudor house, television played and replayed Simpson's endless journey. The next day, the *L.A Times* gave most of the front page and seven other pages to the life, career, alleged crime, and capture of the man. Throughout the night and that day, well-wishers left flowers and messages— "We luv ya, O.J."—before the gates of his home. Others stood in silent vigil and stared. All eyes were on L.A. and would be for the year of the trial. We'd done it again.

THIS IS WHERE I came in. The world media is still massed on our doorstep. The O.J. Simpson Circus of the Century, with all of its attendant clowns and tumblers, is over, but an addendum remains. The father of victim Ron Goldman, haunted by his certainty of Simpson's guilt, has filed a wrongful death suit in civil court, so the show goes on. But then why not? This is bigger than the riots or the fires or the earthquakes or the Menendez Boys or Heidi Fleiss or any of the other calamities that have turned the spotlight on L.A. This is *celebrity,* man, mixed with *mur-der,* the very stuff that makes drama, you'll forgive my phrasing, come alive. Multimillion-dollar book deals have already been made, movies are in the works, and at least one miniseries is rumored. It is already part of Hollywood lore, the way Fatty Arbuckle nosed, or, more appropriately, stomached, his way into the history books: O.J. Simpson, America's swivel-hipped, sweet-smiling Monday Night Hero, being hauled away like so much felonious scum, then rising phoenix-like a year later into the heavenly sunlight.

This isn't the L.A. I came to twenty years ago, all puppy-comfortable and kitty-sweet. It isn't even the L.A. that existed when I began this book. We've become like a David Hockney painting done in hell, a series of angles and facades that conceal chaos. There is no way to describe the city anymore. Anytime I figure I know the place, it changes, like restaurants that vanish overnight, like the mini-malls that spring up where gas stations used to be, like parking structures that swallow whole neighborhoods. We are too complicated to dismiss, too violent not to notice, to powerful to overlook.

With all the change, good and bad, comes an energy that didn't exist in the '70s. Time has collapsed behind us. Easygoing isn't even a memory anymore. We are rocketing around like a people gone mad, heading in every direction at once. It is like we are trapped in one of our own stupid movies and can't get out. We aren't thinking about tomorrow. We are thinking only of surviving today. But that's okay, too, I guess. Today is very big in L.A. There's a lot happening. The world media, drawn to us by calamity, remains, sensing our unpredictability. Like dogs at a slaughterhouse, they wait for another bloody nibble, epitomizing in their growling, restless way everyone's anxious anticipation of the next big feed. We've become the nation's biggest feast.

BUT THERE MAY be hope for us after all. Last night I watched as a local reporter asked a tourist from Maine why she was hanging around O.J.'s home, staring and smiling beatifically. It wasn't because of morbid curiosity or a lust for blood. Someone had spotted an image of Jesus in a tree trunk and she had come there to pray.

If you will excuse me, I'm going out to take a look. Maybe it's really Him this time. I'll stand in front of the tree and say, "Nice to see you, J.C. I've got some favors to ask for a city that is rocking and rolling down a primrose path. . . ."